More Praise for the Smiths' first book, *Houseonomics*.

"There is a lot of wisdom in Gary and Margaret Smith's *Houseonomics* regarding the biggest investment that most people ever make. Anyone considering buying or selling or refinancing a house, determining their net worth or their financial preparedness for retirement should read this book. Reading it would be time well spent for recent college graduates, newly weds, those contemplating moving to a new location and those still renting an apartment. It is so well written that reading it is a joy and yet almost everyone can gain valuable knowledge in the process. The time you take to read this book will be a smart investment indeed. Having taught economics at Stanford for 35 years, I can only wish that more authors were as knowledgeable as the Smiths and wrote this well."

John B. Shoven
Charles R. Schwab Professor
Stanford University

"The Smiths have done their homework, and with their new book you can do yours too—on what, for most families, is the most important investment people ever make. Their careful analysis takes account of important elements of the housing decision that even most so-called professional advisers overlook. And their writing is clear and easy to understand. Their book should help millions of American families."

Benjamin M. Friedman
William Joseph Maier Professor of Political Economy
Harvard University

"When it comes to houses, Americans suffer from a collective bipolar disease. In our manic state, we rush out in droves to buy houses before someone else does. In our depressive state, we hide our eyes when passing a For Sale sign. This book is the therapy we need. Not another book offering get-rich-quick in real estate advice. Not another book proclaiming the imminence of the second coming of the Great Depression. This book charts the right path between housing mania and housing depression, offering wise advice for everyone thinking of make one of life's biggest and scariest decisions—buying that first new home."

Ed Leamer
Director
UCLA Anderson Forecast

"*Houseonomics* is essential reading for anyone considering purchasing a home. It explains why owning a home is the best investment most Americans will ever make, and clearly lays out in everyday language and easy to follow numerical examples all of the financial principles associated with the purchase and sale of residential real estate. The book answers questions such as how to pick the best mortgage, how much money one saves by owning rather than renting, whether remodeling is a good economic investment, how tax breaks, leverage and compounding work together to make homeowners rich, and how to decide if a vacation home can be a good investment. World class economists Margaret and Gary Smith give readers the knowledge and confidence to ignore tainted advice from real estate agents or mortgage brokers, and instead make informed decisions that are in their best interest."

Mike Schimmel
Managing Director
Kayne Anderson Capital Advisors

"Few investors treat housing with this level of thoughtfulness and depth. *Houseonomics* offers an invaluable perspective on housing as an asset, with returns that can be calculated and evaluated when considering home ownership and long term personal portfolio management."

Kristin Horne
Principal
TPG Capital

"The Smiths have written a "just in time" book which will greatly help demystify the disinformation that is rampant about housing and real estate. Their academic backgrounds plus the wisdom of their advice on ownership of property puts them in a unique position to be of great value to the American as well as foreign consumer. This is a "must have" book in my opinion."

Frank Pecarich
investor, author, and management consultant

"Finally there is book that takes a rational and logical look at most people's biggest investment; their home. *Houseonomics* gives homeowners the tools to make decisions based on facts and not speculation."

Charles S. Mizrahi
Managing Partner
CGM Partners

"Homebuying can mean stressful encounters with The Industry: the lenders, agents and lawyers who may not speak what you and I would call English. This book breaks down the Big Decision into small words and digestible concepts. They key is what the Smiths call the "home dividend"—an argument for homeowning and how it can serve your interests, not The Industry's."

Scott Tong
Correspondent
Marketplace public radio

"Recent studies show that more than 98% of all homeowners had gains in the purchase of their home if they have owned it over 5 years. The numbers drop measurably for those who have owned for less than 2 years. *Houseonomics* is among the first books to inform current and future homeowners that owning a home should never be seen as a short term speculative investment but rather a sound long term one. This is a simple to read but powerful reminder of the benefits of homeownership along with useful tips on how to navigate through the process of buying and selling."

Steve Murray
Editor
REAL Trends

"The Smiths' meticulous research supports a completely different approach to building wealth through real estate. *Houseonomics* won't make people an instant millionaires, but it will provide readers with the opportunity for a comfortable retirement. Hosueonomics shows that treating a house first and foremost as a place to live is actually the soundest long term investment. It's a dose of common sense and financial planning that is much needed in today's housing market."

Matthew Haines
Founder
PropertyShark.com

The concept of your house as a multi-faceted financial vehicle, central to most people's lives, is fascinating. And the examples of how people make bad decisions because they don't understand the time value of money—total payments error—are important and compelling.

Greg Karp
author
Living Rich by Spending Smart

Your Home Dividend

Why Buying A Home May Be The Best Investment You'll Ever Make

by Gary Smith and Margaret Smith

ISBN-13: 978-0692579527

ISBN-10: 0692579524

Contents

ACKNOWLEDGMENTS

We are grateful to the John Randolph Haynes and Dora Haynes Foundation for their financial support, to the Brookings Institution for supporting our research and giving us a forum for a stimulating discussion of our conclusions, and to the innumerable real estate amateurs and professionals who have shaped our views of the housing market.

ABOUT THE AUTHORS

Dr. Gary Smith is the Fletcher Jones Professor of Economics at Pomona College. He has published eight college-level textbooks, two trade books, and more than eighty research papers. His research has been featured in various media including *The New York Times*, *The Wall Street Journal*, *The Motley Fool*, *Newsweek*, and *BusinessWeek*, CNBC, and WNYC. Gary was a keynote speaker on real estate at the Brookings Institution in Washington DC and the Mortgage Finance Industry Summit in New York City. His book *Standard Deviations, Flawed Assumptions, Tortured Data, and Other Ways to Lie about Statistic*s, was chosen as a *London Times* Book of the Week. Gary received his BA in Mathematics with Honors from Harvey Mudd College and his PhD in Economics from Yale University.

Dr. Margaret Smith is an author, speaker, coach, trainer, and entrepreneur. She is the founder of EnneaGlobal, a leadership consulting company . She is a Certified Financial Planner, a Registered Investment Advisor, a member of the Financial Planning Association, and a Certified Integral Coach through New Ventures West. Margaret received a PhD in Business Economics from Harvard and a simultaneous BA/MA, summa cum laude, in Economics from Yale. She has published various articles on real estate and finance and has taught at Claremont McKenna College, the Peter F. Drucker Graduate School of Management, and Pomona College.

Introduction

The American Dream is to own your own home, whether it is a log cabin in Oregon, a farmhouse in Iowa, or a penthouse in Manhattan. Our homes are where we eat, sleep, play, love, laugh, and cry. Where we read books, grow tomatoes, and play games. Where we can be alone or with our families. Where we can be ourselves. A home is often the biggest investment that a person will ever make and can be the most profitable one, too. Over the years, millions of ordinary hardworking people have prospered simply by owning the home they live in. They didn't win a lottery or find gold in their backyard. They didn't inherit a million dollars from a long-lost relative. They simply made monthly mortgage payments instead of rent payments. You can, too.

When you are thinking about buying or selling a home, there is a lot to think about. Is now a good time to buy? Should you buy a new home or a fixer upper? Should you make a larger or smaller down payment? Should you trade up or downsize? Should you use a real-estate broker or try to do it yourself? Should you choose a fixed rate or an adjustable rate mortgage? A 30-year or 15-year loan? Should you refinance now that interest rates have fallen? Should you pay off your mortgage early? Should you remodel the kitchen? Is a vacation home worth it? What can you do when you are retired and barely have enough money to buy food, but live in a home worth hundreds of thousands of dollars?   We wrote this book to help you answer these questions—and many more. We want to help you make smart decisions about your home, so that you can enjoy your home and profit from it, too.

This book is not encyclopedic. That would be boring to write and tedious to read. Instead, we put together a collection of useful principles, handy tips, and memorable stories—about things that can really make a difference.

Who's Looking Out for You?

Many profit from other people's homes: the contractors who build and remodel homes, the real estate agents who match buyers and sellers; the bankers who lend money to home buyers; the fund managers who trade mortgages among themselves, the agents who sell homeowner's insurance. They offer you advice on building, remodeling, buying, selling, financing, refinancing, and insuring homes. But their advice is inherently suspect. Are their recommendations for your benefit or theirs?

We don't have any conflicts of interest. We won't make a dime if you buy a home, remodel your kitchen, or choose a 10-year mortgage. Our goal is to give you useful tools and insights that you can use to make informed decisions.

Our Stories

Financial decisions involve some unfamiliar principles. Even professionals make mistakes. So what can we expect from amateurs who will only buy and sell a few homes in their lifetime? A lot! We wrote this book because we know that anyone can learn to make reasonable financial decisions about homeownership. One way to learn how to make smart financial decisions is to identify bad decisions. This book identifies several pitfalls to avoid.

We have included many stories to show you the typical kinds of housing decisions that people face. All our stories are real. We changed the names and some unimportant details to protect the individuals' privacy because these stories are intended to inform, not embarrass. In fact, some of the stories are about mistakes that we ourselves have made.

We have learned from these stories and so can you. Let's get started.

1

The Million-Dollar Question

Your home is your castle, a refuge where you can live securely and comfortably. But your home is also a very important investment, probably the most important investment you will ever make. Your home can make you rich in a way that renting never can. This is why you need to think of your home as an investment.

Imagine for a moment that you are thinking about buying a home and you find the perfect house on a lovely street with beautiful trees. This house isn't the biggest on the street, nor the smallest. Every home in the neighborhood is in good condition: mowed lawns, pruned roses, no barking dogs behind chain-link fences, and no rusted-out cars on blocks. When your realtor showed you the house, several neighbors stopped to chat and they all seemed very friendly.

This house is close to parks, shopping, and your job. The schools have a good reputation and the city has long prided itself on doing what it takes to improve the community and enhance property values—sponsoring youth sports programs, subsidizing activities for adults and senior citizens, having summer concerts in the park, purchasing open spaces, supporting local businesses, and blocking strip-mall blight.

The house is a cute bungalow, with three bedrooms and two baths—just what you have spent months looking for in a home. The modern kitchen is spacious, with a cork floor and granite countertops. The doors are solid hardwood, the windows are double paned, and the ceilings are 10-feet high. The walls and attic are well insulated, which will help lower the heating and air-conditioning bills. The backyard has room for children to play and a sunny spot for a vegetable garden. And this home will look even better with your furniture inside and with a different color of paint on the outside. The asking price is in line with what similar homes are selling for in this area.

Is there anything else to think about? Yes! You need to think about this home as an investment.

First, can you afford it? You have saved money for a down payment, but you're still about $10,000 short. You can possibly borrow some money from relatives, but how will you pay them back and what strings will be attached? Or maybe you can borrow money with one of your credit cards. What about the monthly mortgage payments? It seems like a real stretch, but maybe you can cut back elsewhere: fewer restaurants and no new clothes or vacations for awhile. Or maybe you can use your credit cards to help with the monthly payments as well as the down payment. How do you know if you can really afford to buy a home?

A friendly mortgage broker, Linda, said that she could get you a low interest rate for the first year and the rate probably won't go up much the second year. Plus, Linda said that this home's value will surely go up, so that next year you can use a home equity loan to make your mortgage payments. Is her advice sensible or foolish?

Another consideration is whether this house will be a profitable investment. Linda said that home prices will surely go up. What if she is wrong? Maybe she's optimistic because she wants to lend you money. But why would Linda want to lend you money if you can't pay it back? Is it because she gets a commission if you borrow money from her company?

What if Linda is right and the value of your home does go up every year? How much does it have to go up to make this a good investment? The money you saved for your down payment is invested in stocks and the stock market is doing fine. You saw a smart guy on TV who said that now is a great time to be in the stock market. You saw a smart gal on TV who said that home prices have historically not increased as fast as stock prices. Does that mean that stocks are a better investment than homes?

Yes, homeownership involves a lot more than finding the right house in the right location and painting it the right color. We are going to help you analyze all the questions that you should ask yourself before you buy a home.

Our Homes Are Our Castles

There are many good reasons to own the home you live in. A home is a special place, and it is even more special if your home is really yours.

Your home supports your life. Your yard gives your children a safe place to play. Your home provides a place to entertain your friends. The location of your home determines how far you have to travel to get to work, shopping, and entertainment. If your children go to a great neighborhood school, your home's location makes this possible.

If you own your own home, you don't have to be satisfied with the landlord's choice of paint colors. You don't have to nag the landlord to fix a leaky faucet or sue the landlord to get the moldy carpet replaced. You don't have to pay unconscionable heating bills because of leaky windows and an obsolete furnace. You can add another bedroom, put in a patio, or plant a garden. If you own your own home, you will have more freedom and more privacy.

On the other hand, making a rational decision about something that is so important to you is difficult. Some people don't buy the home they live in because they fear commitment. To them, buying a home seems so permanent, like marrying or having children. Others buy a home and are then paralyzed by the idea that they might buy the wrong furniture or paint their home the wrong color. So, they live with what they have rather than with what they want. And some people get so excited about buying furniture that they fill their homes with so many tables, chairs, sofas, and cabinets that it is a challenge getting from one room to the next. Some are so excited about painting their walls that they create what look to be large-scale replicas of the preschool art normally displayed on refrigerator doors. Still others can't upgrade because it seems wasteful to replace things. "Why do we need a more efficient water heater? The old one still works."

There is nothing wrong with experiencing any of these feelings. One very good reason for buying a home is the emotional pleasure you will derive from being a homeowner. However, if you think of your home as an investment, you will think a little more rationally and a little less emotionally about your home.

An Engine to Prosperity

We have all seen books and infomercials selling advice on how to become a millionaire in a booming housing market (hint: buy low and sell high) or how to become a millionaire in a depressed housing market (hint: buy low and sell high). This "advice" makes sense, but if it is so easy, then why do these people spend so much time and effort selling advice when they could be flipping homes instead?

Our advice is quite different and, unlike the infomercial pitchmen, we definitely follow our own advice. We own the home we live in. You should, too, if the numbers make sense. You don't have to be a speculator or a slumlord to get rich. You can become a millionaire simply by owning your home. This is great news because most people would not be happy being speculators or slumlords, but will be very happy living in their own homes.

After the 2000–2003 dot-com crash in the stock market, many people jumped into the real estate game. Some bought foreclosed properties. Some rehabbed fixer-uppers. Some accumulated rental properties. When home prices are rising rapidly, speculators can make money pretty easily by flipping homes—buying homes and selling them a few months, weeks, or even days later for a quick profit. Oddly enough, although many people are familiar with the idea of flipping homes, they don't think about their own home—the home they live in—as an engine to prosperity. They say, "Everyone has to live somewhere, right? My home is not a real investment like stocks and bonds. It is just where I live."

No, your home is an incredibly important investment. Your home is not a lottery ticket—don't buy a home thinking that it will make you rich overnight. Your home is not a brokerage account—don't day trade homes (or stocks, for that matter). Your home is not an ATM—don't use home equity loans to buy things you don't need. Your home is an investment that can make you rich and that you can enjoy all your life if you make prudent, sensible financial decisions about your purchase, your mortgage, and your remodeling.

You can think of your home as a retirement account, like an Individual Retirement Account (IRA). Let's call it a Home Retirement Account (HRA). Ordinary retirement accounts have great tax advantages. So does your home. Ordinary retirement accounts can provide financial security for you when you are retired. So can your home.

Homes are different from stocks in that you can't really enjoy your stocks much beyond watching their prices fluctuate daily. (Is that fun or scary?) But you can enjoy your home. You can live in your home. You can paint the walls and rearrange the furniture. You can remodel. You can take pride in being a homeowner.

In this book, we show you how to think about your home as an investment, indeed as an HRA.

Uncle Sam Wants You to Be a Homeowner

The average renter in the United States has less than $5,000 in wealth. The average homeowner has nearly $200,000, which is 40 times as much wealth as a renter. Is this because homeowners earn 40 times what renters earn? No. Homeowners, on average, earn about twice as much as renters, $50,000 a year versus $25,000 a year. The main reason homeowners are 40 times wealthier than renters is because they are homeowners! Most of their wealth is their home and they built up this wealth by owning instead of renting. For most people, the easiest way to become wealthy is to become a homeowner. It really is as simple as that.

Several government subsidies and tax breaks make it easy and profitable to become a homeowner. Three of the most important ones are:

1. You don't pay taxes on the income you get from your home.
2. You pay minimal taxes on the profit you make when you sell your home.
3. You can deduct your mortgage interest from your taxable income.

Let's look at these three incentives one by one.

Most people don't know about the first incentive, which is usually the most important of the three. If you have a savings account or a stock portfolio, your income is the interest and dividends you earn and you have to pay taxes on this income. If you own a home, you have income too, but it is harder to see and it goes untaxed.

The income from your home is the rent you save by being a homeowner. If you are a renter and pay $1,500 a month to rent a home, this is $1,500 that you no longer have. If you own this home instead of renting it, you keep the $1,500 that you don't pay in rent each month. This $1,500 is real cash that you can put in your bank account instead of your landlord's pocket—and you don't pay a penny of taxes on it. Later in this book, when we examine how owning a home builds your wealth, you will see that this untaxed income is the secret that can make you rich.

The second incentive is that you pay minimal taxes when you sell your home. If you sell a stock for more than you paid for it, your profit is called a capital gain and you have to pay a capital gains tax on your profit. Homeowners, however, get a big tax break. If you live in your home for at least two of the five years before you sell it, your profit is not taxed up to $250,000 if you are single or up to $500,000 if you are married.

At the current 15 percent capital gains tax rate, if you sell stock for a $500,000 profit (just pretend!), you pay a $75,000 tax. If you are married and sell your home for a $500,000 profit, you don't pay any capital gains tax. If you sell your home for more than a $500,000 profit, you pay a tax on the excess, but please don't complain if you make more than a $500,000 profit on your home!

The third incentive is that your mortgage interest is tax-deductible. Suppose you have a $200,000 mortgage at a 6 percent interest rate. In the first year, your mortgage payments will be $14,900, of which about $12,000 is interest. You can report this interest on your federal tax return as an itemized deduction and it might reduce your taxable income by $12,000. (We say "might" because of the standard deduction, alternative minimum tax, and other complexities of the tax code). If you are in a 25 percent tax bracket, you will save $3,000 in taxes. That's right. Uncle Sam will pay a quarter of your interest payments for you. Why? Because the government wants to encourage you to do the right thing and become a homeowner.

What about the $2,900 of your mortgage payment that is not interest? This $2,900 is a "principal payment" that pays down your mortgage. Because principal payments reduce your mortgage, they also reduce the interest you owe on your mortgage. If you have a 6 percent mortgage, every dollar reduction in your mortgage is a dollar you no longer have to pay 6 percent interest on. Therefore, paying down your mortgage is an investment that earns a 6 percent return.

This remarkable fact bears repeating because it is not well known. Think of your home as a special bank account and think of your principal payments as bank deposits. Your principal payments are savings that build up equity in your home, the same way that savings deposited in a bank build up your bank account. Paying down a mortgage with a 6 percent interest rate is an investment with a 6 percent return.

Mortgage payments are not just interest on your loan, they are also investing. This is forced investing because you have to do it— you have to make your mortgage payments or the bank will foreclose. For many people, this is another advantage of buying a home. It forces them to save money when they might otherwise not be sufficiently disciplined to do so.

The Million-Dollar Question

Yes, there are many benefits from home ownership. But there are costs, too. We didn't write this book for dreamers who think real estate will make them rich overnight. This book is for people who are going to love in their homes for many years. They do not need get-rich-quick schemes that are literally too good to be true. They need to know whether the benefits exceed the costs.

We hear two kinds of concerns about buying a home. The first is, "Home prices are too high." This usually means that home prices are higher than they were many years ago, which may be because home prices in the past were too low! What we mean is that in most places, homes were a bargain in that homeowners made a great investment—often the best investment in their whole life.

The million-dollar question is whether, at today's prices, a home is still a good investment. In most places, the answer is yes. We are not saying that you should buy a home no matter what the price. You need to be able to identify the firm ground and the quicksand. We will show you how.

The second concern we hear is, "Real estate prices aren't booming where I live." For example, an Indianapolis resident told us that Indianapolis was a bad place to buy a home because home prices there only go up 2 percent to 3 percent a year. We are going to show you that Indianapolis is a great place to be a homeowner even if home prices don't go up *at all*. And there are lots of similar cities all over this country—wonderful places to live where home prices don't have to go up for homes to be good investments.

Both of these concerns—that home prices are higher than they used to be and that home prices might only go up a few percent a year—tell us that home buyers are asking the wrong question. Instead of looking at how much home prices have increased, or are increasing, homebuyers should be looking at something quite different, what we call the *home dividend*. If you look at your home dividend, you may find that a home is well worth owning— not because home prices are going to increase rapidly but because your home dividend is your engine to prosperity.

Slow and Steady Wins the Race

Anne and Mary grew up together in Wisconsin. They lived on the same street, went to the same schools, and have been lifelong friends. They are now 39 years old, but there has been one really important difference in their lives. Anne bought a house when she was 21. Seven years later, she sold this house and bought an even bigger one. Now she is living in a house that is worth $420,000. She still has a $118,000 mortgage, but she could sell her home and walk away with $300,000. Mary never bought a house. She has been paying rent for 18 years and all she has to show for it is a shoebox full of hundreds of rent receipts.

Over the past 18 years, Mary paid rent and Anne made mortgage payments and it hasn't been easy for either of them. They spent roughly the same amount on food, shelter, clothing, and entertainment and had roughly the same standard of living. But Anne has built up equity in her home and Mary has collected rent receipts. Now Anne is living in a half-million dollar home that will soon be paid for and Mary will most likely go on paying rent for the rest of her life because she can't afford to make a down payment on a house at today's prices.

Anne didn't find a winning lottery ticket. Like millions of people all across this great country, she built her wealth slowly but surely by paying off the mortgage on her home one month at a time.

The Bottom Line

1. Your home is your castle, especially if you own your home.
2. Your home can be a major engine to prosperity—if you own your home.
3. Your home is not a lottery ticket, a speculative bet, or an ATM.
4. Renting can't make you rich; owning the home you live in can make you a millionaire.

Your Home is an Investment

What is your home really worth? Buyers, sellers, realtors, and appraisers all focus on comps, which are the prices of comparable homes. If the house next door sold for $300,000, then your house is evidently worth $300,000. We disagree.

To decide what a home is really worth, you need to think of a home as an investment. A home is worth $300,000 if it is a good investment at that price. If it isn't a good investment at that price, then be skeptical, very skeptical, even if similar homes have recently sold for $300,000.

Investment Versus Speculation

A few years ago, people paid hundreds of dollars for stuffed animals known as Beanie Babies. Is a Beanie Baby worth $500 just because somebody paid $500 for it? Beanie Babies like the one shown in Figure 2.1 sold for $500 several years ago; now you can buy them for less than $5. What were people thinking when they paid hundreds of dollars for a Beanie Baby? Were they thinking that their children would have so much fun playing with a Beanie Baby that it was well worth $500? No, they thought they were planning to get rich by "investing" in Beanie Babies.

They weren't really investing. They were speculating—speculating that they would be able to sell their $500 Beanie Baby for $1,000. This type of speculation is called the greater fool theory: you buy something at an inflated price, hoping to sell it to an even bigger fool for a still higher price.

Real investors, like Warren Buffett, don't count on selling their investments for a profit. They count on the income from their investment. When real investors buy a stock, it is not because they expect the stock's price to be higher tomorrow than it is today, but rather because they expect the company's earnings and dividends to provide a good return on their investment. Suppose, for example, that a stock pays a dividend of $10 a year, every year, forever. If you buy this stock for $100, then the $10 annual dividend gives you a 10 percent return on your investment. You don't have to sell the stock for a higher price for this to be a good investment.

The question that real investors ask is not what the price will be tomorrow (which is impossible to know, anyway), but whether the income from the investment is high enough to justify the price. A $100 stock that pays a $10 annual dividend is a good investment. A Beanie Babies that pays no income is a bad investment.

Think of your home as an investment. First and foremost, this means don't think like a Beanie-Baby speculator. Don't buy a home because you think you will be able to sell it for a profit. Do buy a home because you think that the income from your home will provide a good return on your investment.

Figure 2.1 Is this Beanie Baby Worth $500?

Your Home Dividend

What is the income from a home? In 2007, a *New York Times* writer couldn't figure it out. He said that "houses have no underlying revenue stream (such as a stock's corporate earnings) on which to base an assumption of true value." He is wrong. Homes do have income. It is a subtle principle, but it is absolutely crucial for understanding why a home can be a great investment.

If you are a landlord who rents a home to someone else, the income is obvious—the rent check you get each month from your tenant. If you own a home and live in it, there is income, too; but it is harder to see because no one hands you a check each month. The income is the rent check you don't have to give to someone else. When you write a rent check for $1,500, this money goes out of your bank account and into your landlord's bank account. If you own your home, the $1,500 doesn't leave your bank account. This $1,500 is not an abstract theoretical $1,500. It is a real $1,500 that you can invest or use to buy food, clothing, and entertainment. This $1,500 is income from your home.

Of course, there are other financial benefits from home ownership (including the tax deductibility of your interest payments and property taxes), and there are also expenses associated with owning a home, including the monthly mortgage payments, property taxes, and maintenance. Table 2.1 shows some hypothetical numbers.

Table 2.1 Your Annual Home Dividend

Income and Expenses	Dollar Amount
Rent savings	$18,000
Mortgage payment	−$8,000
Property tax	−$3,000
Tax savings	$2,500
Insurance	−$500
Maintenance	−$3,000
Home dividend	$6,000

Don't worry about the specific numbers in Table 2.1. In Chapter 3, "Now Is a Good Time to Own a Home," you will see some real numbers for real homes. For now, just think about the general idea that your home gives you income, just like other investments.

By owning your own home, you are able to save the rent money you would otherwise have to pay to a landlord. On the other hand, you have to make mortgage payments and pay property taxes on your home. These will be offset to some extent by the fact that you can deduct them from your taxable income and thereby reduce your income taxes. Finally, you will have to pay for homeowner's insurance and for maintenance expenses when faucets drip and the walls need to be repainted.

The bottom line in Table 2.1 is $6,000 a year, or $500 a month. If you own this home instead of renting it, you will have an extra $500 a month in your bank account. Because this money is as real as the dividends from a stock portfolio, we call it your home dividend. Your home dividend is cash that you can spend or invest. In Chapter 3, we show you how to calculate your own home dividend.

The most important component of your home dividend is the rent savings. You can usually get a pretty good idea of the rent savings by looking at rental ads in the newspaper or on the Internet. In every city there are lots of very similar homes in close proximity to each other—some of which are for sale and some of which are for rent. Sometimes, you can find virtually identical homes that are adjacent to each other or across the street from each other.

For example, Figures 2.2 and 2.3 show two single-family homes across the street from each other in Diamond Bar, California, a residential city in Los Angeles County. Both houses are 1,812 square-feet, 4-bedroom, 2-bath, split-level homes that were built in 1964. One family bought the house in Figure 2.2; another family rented the house in Figure 2.3. The family that bought the house could look across the street to get a pretty good estimate of the rent they saved when they became homeowners.

Figure 2.2 This house was purchased

Figure 2.3 The house across the street was rented

If you can buy or rent very similar properties (perhaps even the same property), then the financial question is whether the home dividends (the rent savings and tax benefits minus the mortgage payment and other expenses) are large enough to justify being a homeowner. There are surely also nonfinancial considerations that make renting and owning different. Renters might not like the pumpkin orange walls the landlord picked out. Renters don't get any financial benefit from remodeling a kitchen or landscaping a yard. Renters might have less privacy than they would have if they owned their home. These are all arguments for why owning is better than renting and, to the extent they matter, home-dividend calculations underestimate the value of homeownership.

There are two important takeaways. First, don't speculate—in stocks or in real estate—by trying to guess short-term price changes; instead, look at the potential income. Second, the investment value of a home is determined by the home dividends, not by comps. Comps cannot tell you if a home is really worth the price. Home dividends can tell you this.

We are definitely not saying that you can't go wrong buying a home, no matter what the price. Everything has a price that is too low and a price that is too high. An orange is a bargain at a penny and too expensive at $100. We are encouraging you to look at the home dividends before you buy so that you can judge for yourself whether a home is really worth the price.

The Nifty Fifty

In the early 1970s, investors were in love with the Nifty Fifty—a small group of stocks so appealing that they should always be bought and never sold. Among these select few were IBM, Xerox, Disney, McDonald's, Avon, and Polaroid. Each was a leader in its field, with a strong balance sheet and rapidly growing earnings.

What were these Nifty stocks worth? Investors simply compared the prices of the Nifty stocks to each other. If the price of Avon stock is 60 times Avon's earnings per share, then it is reasonable that Xerox's stock price is 60 times Xerox's earnings. They were using comps to value stocks!

This eagerness to buy as long as the prices are comparable virtually guarantees that these prices will eventually be too high. There was a Nifty Fifty bubble that popped. Avon fell from $140 in 1973 to $19 in 1974. Polaroid fell from $150 to $14, Xerox from $172 to $49.

Comps are just comps. They don't tell you what something is really worth.

Waiting to Buy

Michael Keene, a professor of economics, had been living with his family in university-subsidized faculty housing for several years. Then, in 2003, his university decided that it was another professor's turn to live in this house. The Keenes had to move out.

The Keenes looked around for another place to live and found the perfect house (just the right size, cute as could be, and close to work and their children's schools). The owner was offering to rent this house for $2,000 a month or sell it for $450,000.

The Keenes remembered that houses like this used to sell for $250,000 and, besides, they had read in a newspaper that home prices were 20 percent too high, whatever that meant. So, they decided to rent until the price of this house fell 20 percent, to $360,000. They are still waiting. But now houses like this sell for more than $600,000 and they can't afford to buy their perfect house.

Some people say that buying a house is risky. Not buying is risky, too.

It Is Hard to Time the Housing Market

Unlike the Keenes, the Robinsons owned a home in 2003— a house they bought years ago for $100,000. They watched with increasing joy as home prices went up and up and up. They took a beating when they bought dot-com stocks at their peak in the spring of 2000, but the rising value of their home helped offset the falling value of their stocks.

Then they started reading newspaper stories and seeing television reports about a housing bubble. They became convinced that housing prices were about to collapse. They decided to sell their home for $480,000 before the price went back down to $100,000. In 2003, they sold their home and rented an apartment, convinced that they could buy back their home cheaply after the bubble popped. Then they watched with dismay as home prices kept rising. In 2007, their home had a market value of $720,000, nearly double what they had sold it for in 2003. They couldn't afford to buy back their home! So, they kept paying rent and hoping that home prices would collapse. As of 2015, they are still waiting, and still paying a landlord rent every month.

Taking the Long View

The Robinsons and the Keenes tried to predict short-term changes in home prices and they guessed wrong. They should have been thinking about home dividends instead.

Suppose that you live in an area for 60 years. And suppose that you change houses every 10 or 15 years. You marry and divorce. You have children and your children grow up. You change jobs and you change. For whatever reasons, you might own four or five different homes during these 60 or so years. Ups and downs in home prices during these 60 years aren't all that important. If you sell your home for a much higher price than you paid for it, you will pay a high price for your new home. If you sell your home when prices are low, you will buy your next home for a low price. Over long horizons like this, the income you get from owning your home—your home dividend—will usually be much more important than wiggles and jiggles in home prices. So, don't fret about short-term zigs and zags in home prices; instead, focus on whether the prospective home dividends over many years justify current home prices.

Once you focus on years and years of home dividends, a home is not as risky an investment as you might think. While buying a home might seem risky, not buying is risky, too. If you wait too long to buy, you might get priced out of the housing market and have to pay rent for the rest of your life. Or think of it this way. You don't have to buy stocks. But you do need a place to live— which you can pay for with rent or with mortgage payments.

Which do you think is riskier: making mortgage payments that are constant or making rent payments that can change every year? (If you have an adjustable rate mortgage, then your mortgage payments may change, too, but that is another issue, which we address in Chapter 6, "Choosing the Right Mortgage.")

Home prices won't ever collapse the way the prices of Beanie Babies and dot-com stock plummeted because homes are fundamentally different from Beanie Babies and dot-com stocks. Homes have a substantial income—home dividends—that Beanie Babies and flimsy dot-com stocks never had. When the prices of Beanie Babies and dot-com stocks started falling, there was no longer any reason to buy them. If home prices fall dramatically, there is a very good reason to buy a home—to get the home dividends! Like many a great investor has said, if you like a stock at $50, you will love it at $40. If you like a home at $300,000, you will love it at $200,000.

Don't try to time the stock market and don't try to time the real estate market. Just keep your eye on the home dividends. If the numbers make sense, buy a home that you will love living in and don't fret about short-term wiggles and jiggles in home prices. Warren Buffett has famously advised, "Only buy something that you'd be perfectly happy to hold if the market shut down for 10 years." For real estate, this means only buy a house if you would be happy to live in it for ten years.

Don't Day Trade Homes

Not long ago, if you wanted to buy or sell a stock, you telephoned your broker to get a current price and to pass your instructions along to the firm's traders. Oftentimes, the broker called you to suggest a trade. The broker's commission was equal to around 2 percent of the value of the trade; for example, if you bought 500 shares of stock at $20 a share (a $10,000 trade), you paid a commission of around $200. These high commissions made short-term trading expensive and it was rare for an individual to buy and sell a stock on the same day.

Then two things happened. First, deregulation and competition reduced commissions drastically, with some online brokerage firms charging commissions of less than $10 for trades that used to cost hundreds of dollars. Second, personal computers with access to the Internet allowed individuals to monitor stock prices continuously. These revolutionary developments lured some dreamers into becoming compulsive traders—sitting in front of their computers for hours and jumping in and out of the market, buying a stock because the price dipped (or jumped) with the hope that they could sell it a short while later for a profit. This frenetic activity was aided and abetted by the dot-com bubble—it is hard not to make money when stock prices are going up by 40 percent a year.

This hyperactive trading is commonly referred to as *day trading*, because day traders might make dozens or even hundreds of trades in a day. Many day traders borrow large amounts of money to make large wagers that can be very profitable, or disastrous.

After the dot-com meltdown, day trading stocks became less profitable and less popular. Ever hopeful of making easy money, some day traders turned to gold, currencies, and other speculative gambles. One of the more interesting developments is the day trading of foreign currencies by middle-income Japanese housewives, often without the knowledge of their husbands. In 2007, online currency trading by Japanese individuals averaged nearly $10 billion a day, a fifth of all currency trading worldwide.

The real estate market has also been a magnet for people who have more dreams than common sense. If you can buy a home for $200,000 and sell it a short while later for $250,000, that is more money than you can earn in a year in many tedious, dead-end jobs. Why not buy and sell homes so that you can quit your awful job? Why not pay a motivational speaker thousands of dollars to learn how to play the real estate game? Why not, indeed.

These home traders are called house flippers because they buy a home not to live in, but to sell a short while later for a profit. House flippers are not literally day traders— they seldom buy and sell a home in the same day—but they are like day traders in that they are compulsive, short-term traders who hope to profit from short-term price movements.

When home prices rise at double-digit rates in an area, people can make money by flipping homes. As with dot-com stocks, making money is easy when prices are rising rapidly. And as with dot-com stocks, the profits vanish when prices stop rising rapidly. Even with low commissions, most stock-market day traders lose money. House flipping is even more hazardous to your wealth because the trading costs are so high. If you buy a home for a year, the mortgage interest, property taxes, real estate commissions, legal fees, and other expenses can easily add up to more than 10 percent of the value of the home. If this home's price goes up by only 3 percent, not at all, or (heaven forbid) falls, house flipping can bankrupt you. Many people who made millions flipping homes also lost millions.

We didn't write this book to persuade you to flip homes you will never live in. This book is for people who either already live in their own home or want to buy a home to live in. We want o help you better understand how to turn your home into an engine of prosperity. The key to this engine of prosperity is your home dividends, not house flipping.

Your Home Is an Investment

Some people don't consider their home as part of their wealth. They say, "Everyone has to live somewhere, right?" Yes, everyone has to live somewhere. But you can choose to be a renter or an owner—to pay a landlord or to pay off a mortgage. A home is a place to live, but it is also an investment.

"But I will never sell my home and live in the street; so, my home isn't really valuable like stocks and bonds." You don't have to sell your home for it to be a valuable investment. If your mortgage payments (and other expenses) are less than what you would pay in rent, then your home is paying you a home dividend every month. When your mortgage is paid off, you will be living in a home mortgage free and saving thousands of dollars in rent. All this money you don't pay to a landlord is money that you can invest or spend on food, clothing, entertainment, whatever you want. Yes, your home is valuable like stocks and bonds.

A Home to Call Their Own

Mary and George Walters are in their early 60s and have paid off the mortgage on their home—a half-acre oasis in the middle of a suburban sprawl of tract homes and strip malls. They have a productive garden and dozens of mature fruit trees, a backyard studio and kiln for George's pottery making, and a lovely patio where they drink wine and watch the sunset. They could sell their home for $600,000, but they won't. They've made this home their own and plan to live in it until they die.

Their home is a valuable investment even though they won't sell it. They pay a few thousand dollars a year in property taxes and maintenance, but that's it. If they didn't own their home they would have to pay around $2,500 a month to rent a similar house (and it wouldn't have a pottery studio and kiln!). Their home is saving them $30,000 a year in rent, and rents will almost surely keep going up over time. If rents rise by 3 percent a year, their annual rental savings will be $40,000 in 10 years and $54,000 in 20 years. Their home is like a money machine that spits out $30,000 this year and 3 percent more every year thereafter.

This money machine is a valuable part of their wealth. George was able to quit his job teaching at a junior high school and work on his true passion, pottery, because the Walters own their home and George doesn't need to go to work to pay the rent. Mary kept working because she liked her job and the health insurance that came with it, but she could afford to quit, too—and she did when they were old enough to qualify for Medicare. Now she pursues her passion—photography.

Look at the Whole Picture

If you are the kind of person who keeps track of your wealth, then you should include your home in your calculations. It doesn't have to be an exact number, correct to the last penny, but it can be a reasonable estimate. Make sure you calculate your equity in your house, not the total value of the house. Your equity is what you would walk away with if you sold your home and paid off your mortgage. If you have a mortgage balance of $100,000 and you sell your home for $300,000, then your equity is $200,000.

Overall, Americans have more wealth in their homes than in their stocks and bonds. How can you think seriously about how much wealth you have and how it is invested, if you don't include your most important investment?

What Am I Supposed to Look at Again?

Amy and Rick Williams sold their home in 2003 and walked away with more than $300,000 in cash. They bought a new home for $400,000 by making a $300,000 down payment and borrowing $100,000. In 2005, they took out a $100,000 home-equity loan, which they used to pay off some credit-card debt and do a major remodeling project, including the addition of another bedroom and bathroom.

Amy thought they were managing their finances poorly because they had $100,000 in mortgage in 2003 and $200,000 in 2006.

The reality is that the market value of their home had increased from $400,000 to $600,000 during this three-year period, in part because of their remodeling project. They used some of their borrowed money to make their home more valuable. They also paid off their credit-card debt, and that was smart.

Their mortgage debt had gone up by $100,000; the value of their home had increased by $200,000; and the value of their equity had increased by $100,000. Should they be:

a. Depressed, because their debt increased by $100,000?

b. Ecstatic, because the value of their home increased by $200,000?

c. Happy, because the value of their equity increased by $100,000?

Give yourself full credit if you answered (c).

The Bottom Line

1. Comps tell you what comparable homes sold for, but not what they are really worth.
2. The investment value of a home depends on its home dividend: the rent savings plus the tax benefits minus the mortgage payments, property taxes, and other expenses.
3. In the long run, home dividends are usually more important than ups and downs in home prices.
4. You have to live somewhere and fixed mortgage payments are less risky than volatile rent payments.
5. Don't try to time the housing market. Don't buy a home because you expect the price to go up; buy a home because the home dividends will give you a good rate of return on your investment.

3

Now is a Good Time to Own a Home

During the 2000–2005 run-up in home prices in the United States, stories appeared in newspapers, magazines, and on television about house flippers—people with big grins and fistfuls of cash who were buying homes in hot markets, hoping to sell them for a big profit a short while later. They never intended to live in these homes, just flip them for a profit. Sometimes, they bought several homes under construction, hoping to resell them before the homes were completed. We didn't write this book for such speculators.

We wrote this book for people like you, who plan to live in your home for many years and want to know if homeownership is likely to be profitable in the long run. For most people in most places, now is a good time to own a home! If you own a home already, congratulations. If you don't yet own a home, you should think about buying one. Twenty years from now, you will probably look back and say that this was the best purchase you ever made.

We can confidently make that statement even though we don't know what your home's price will be 20 years from now. People who think that home prices have to increase rapidly for a home to be a great investment are wrong. It is the home dividends that will make your home a great investment. This chapter explains why and shows you how to estimate your home dividends.

A Home in Fishers, Indiana

In the summer of 2005, Marty and Marie Nelson bought a 3-bedroom, 3-bath, 1,917 square-foot house in Fishers, Indiana, for $135,000 with a 20 percent down payment and a 30-year mortgage. Fishers is an attractive Indianapolis suburb. The average household income is around $90,000 and, almost every year, Fishers is ranked among the top places to live in the United States.

To learn how to determine the home dividends for your own home, pretend you are considering buying this house in Fishers. First, make a list of the annual benefits and expenses from homeownership. Don't include the price of the house, down payment, or closing costs. Just list the annual benefits and expenses. Your list should include the rent savings, mortgage payments, property taxes, the tax savings from the tax deductibility of mortgage interest and property taxes, homeowner's insurance instead of renter's insurance, any utilities you would have to pay as owners that you wouldn't have to pay as renters, and maintenance.

Table 3.1 shows a list of these items and some estimated dollar values. (Appendix A, "An Owner-Occupied Home in Fishers, Indiana." explains in detail how we came up with these numbers.) The biggest benefit is the rent saving; the biggest expense is the mortgage payment.

The bottom line is a first-year home dividend of $5,622. The home dividend is positive because the rent savings and tax savings are larger than the mortgage payment and other expenses. Let's say it one more time. This $5,622 home dividend is real cash. After one year, you will have $5,622 more in your bank account than you would have if you were renting. Just like a stock portfolio that pays a $5,622 dividend, this $5,622 is your home's dividend.

Table 3.1 After-Tax Home Dividend for a Home in Fishers

Income and Expenses	Dollar Amount
Rent savings	$15,000
Mortgage payment	−$7,522
Property tax	−$2,619
Tax savings	$2,447
Insurance	−$334
Utilities	$0
Maintenance	−$1,350
Home dividend	$5,622

Is $5,622 a good return on your investment? Just like with stocks, you should compare the dividend with the size of your investment. When you buy a home, your investment is the amount of cash you put up as your down payment. Here, your down payment is assumed to be $27,000, or 20 percent of the price. To buy this home, you invested $27,000, which you could have otherwise invested in stocks or a money-market fund or whatever you choose. The $5,622 first-year home dividend is equal to 21 percent of your $27,000 down payment. Your home dividend gives you a 21 percent after-tax rate of return on your investment! Where else could you invest $27,000 and get a $5,622 dividend the first year?

Figure 3.1 shows that your home dividend will get bigger each year because rents will increase, but your mortgage payments will not (if you have a fixed rate mortgage). Your home dividend will be $5,942 in the second year, $8,843 the tenth year, $13,471 the twentieth year, and $19,478 the thirtieth year. Then the mortgage payments stop and your home dividend jumps to $27,118 in the thirty-first year, and keeps on growing. What a great investment!

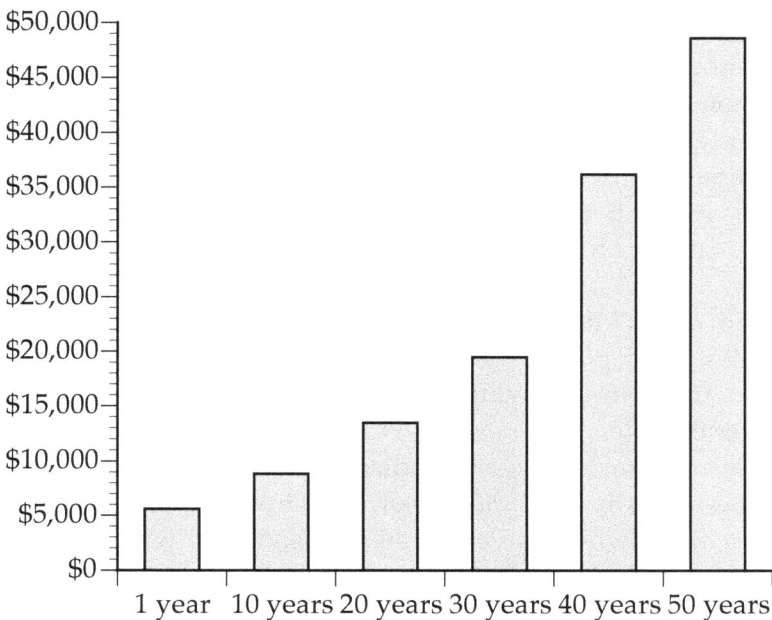

Figure 3.1 Your home dividend grows over time

Warren Buffett has said that his "favorite holding period is forever." Even though no one lives forever, it is a superb idea to value an investment by assuming that it will never be sold, because that removes the temptation to speculate on price fluctuations. If an investment is held forever, all that matters is the income from the investment. For a home purchase, all that matters is the home dividend.

When we assume an infinite holding period for this home in Fishers, the implicit after-tax rate of return works out to be 28 percent. The long-run 28-percent return is higher than the first-year 21-percent return because the home dividend grows each year as the rent saving increases relentlessly while the mortgage expense is fixed for 30 years and then stops. Remember, this 28-percent return calculation is just valuing the annual home dividend; it makes no assumptions about the future price of the home.

The home dividend does not include the expenses you incur when you buy or sell a home (realtor's commission and other closing costs) because these are not annual expenses. These expenses are often large enough to destroy your profits if you only own the home a short while. Suppose that these expenses amount to 7 percent of the home's price. This 7 percent cost is likely to eat up your home dividend if you only stay in the house for a year or two. In this example, 7 percent of $135,000 is $9,450, which is more than the first-year dividend. The only way you can make a profit after one year is if the price of the house goes up, which you shouldn't count on. Remember, you aren't a home-flipping speculator.

A good rule of thumb to follow is that you shouldn't buy a home unless you plan to stay in it for at least 5 to 7 years. Otherwise, the costs of buying and selling are usually too high to make it worthwhile.

For this house in Fishers, Indiana, the fundamentals look great. Unless you have some reason to think that rents will go down over time (which is very unlikely), someone who plans to live in Fishers for a long time is likely to profit handsomely from buying this house.

You can apply what you learned from this example to homes anywhere.

1. Estimate the home dividend. The most appealing situations are those where the home dividend is positive the very first year.
2. The ratio of the first-year home dividend to the down payment is an estimate of your first-year after-tax rate of return; in this example, $5,622 / $27,000 = 0.21(21 percent).
3. If rents increase over time and your mortgage payments do not, then your home dividend is going to increase as time passes.
4. The cost of buying and selling homes is substantial. A home purchase is more likely to be profitable if you plan to live in the home for several years.

All real estate is local. You can't tell whether your home or a home you are thinking about buying is like this home in Fishers, Indiana, until you look at the numbers. However, there is something really interesting about the Fishers example that was mentioned earlier in this book.

Remember the Indianapolis resident who told us that he didn't think Indianapolis was a good place to buy a home because real estate prices there only go up by 2% to 3% a year? He is wrong.

The price of this home in Fishers happened to increase by about 1% a year over the next ten years, to $150,000 in 2015, but we weren't counting on that. Our home-dividend calculation assumed *zero* price increase and the home was still a profitable investment.

His mistake—and it is a common one—is to focus on the price appreciation and ignore the home dividends. If you buy a home, buy it for the home dividends. A home can be a great investment because of the great dividends.

We have looked at dozens of homes in the Indianapolis area and hundreds of homes all over the country and found that the home dividends provide a very attractive return even if home prices don't increase. Lots of cities all over the country have homes that are well worth the price.

Cash is King

Why was this home in Fishers, Indiana, such a great investment? Because of the large home dividends: the rent savings plus tax benefits minus the mortgage payments and other expenses. In our Fishers example, the first-year home dividend was equal to 21 percent of the down payment and the home dividend will grow over time.

To illustrate, suppose that rents and home prices in Fishers go up by 3 percent a year over the next 30 years and that the home dividends earn a 5 percent return. Remember, these home dividends are real money, cash you can invest because you a homeowner instead of a renter, making mortgage payments instead of rent payments.

You invest the first-year $5,622 home dividend and continue to invest your future home dividends every year. You will be a millionaire by the time your last mortgage payment is made, with $700,000 in the bank and a home that is worth $300,000. That's right. You invest $27,000 by buying a home to live in. Rents and home prices go up by a modest 3 percent a year and your home dividends earn a modest 5 percent return. Even with these conservative assumptions, your $27,000 investment will make you a millionaire in 30 years.

After that last mortgage payment, your wealth grows even faster because your rent savings keep on growing and you no longer have to make mortgage payments. Your wealth will be $1.9 million after 40 years and $3.5 million after 50 years. Your annual after-tax rate of return is 13 percent over 30 years, 14 percent over 40 years, and 15 percent over 50 years.

We are going to repeat this conclusion because it is so important. You buy a home to live in and get home dividends equal to your rent savings and tax benefits minus your mortgage payments and other expenses. The market price of your home goes up by 3 percent a year and you invest your annual home dividends in a bank account that pays 5 percent interest. Your long-run, after-tax, rate of return is 13% to 15%. Where are you going to find another investment that gives you such a wonderful return? And where are you going to find an investment that gives you as much pleasure as the home you live in?

The "secret" behind these miraculous numbers is the home dividends. People who fixate on price appreciation—believing that the only way to make money in real estate is if prices skyrocket—miss the whole point. A great home dividend is what makes a home a great investment.

Figure 3.2 shows how this Fishers home builds your wealth over time, tracking both your home dividends and the value of your home equity. Most of the payoff comes from the home dividends, not the increase in the price of the home. The home price grows from $135,000 to $300,000 in 30 years. The annual dividends, invested at 5 percent, grow to $700,000. After 30 years, 70 percent of your wealth is from the accumulated dividends. Once the mortgage is paid off, the home dividend is even more important. The invested dividends are 78 percent of your wealth after 40 years and 84 percent after 50 years. This is why you should invest your home dividends every year. Home dividends that earn interest are your engine to prosperity!

Remember, you don't have to live in one home all your life for your home dividends to make you rich. Just be a homeowner all your life. You might live in four, five, or even more homes during your lifetime. As long as your homes pay you a home dividend that you invest year after year, you will get rich.

You can discipline yourself to invest your home dividend by opening a bank account, mutual fund, or brokerage account that you call your "home dividend account." You can even make automatic deposits by having your employer make a direct deposit each month. Then sit back in the home you love and watch your home dividend account grow!

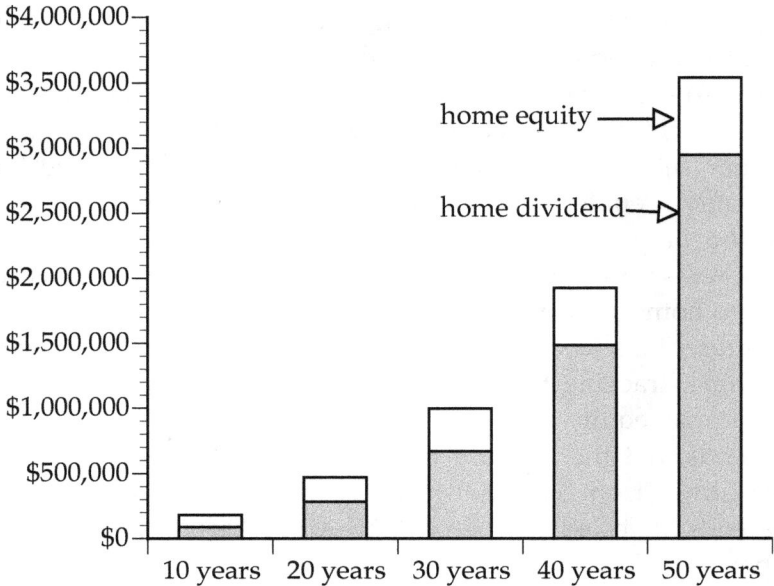

Figure 3.2 Your home is a great investment
because of the home dividends

The calculations in Figure 3.2 assume that you earn a 5 percent return on your home dividends. You will do even better if you invest in the stock market and it happens to earn 10 percent a year, as it has done historically. Now you will have $1.8 million after 30 years, $4.7 million after 40 years, and $12.3 million after 50 years. Of your $1.8 million in total wealth after 30 years, 82 percent is from the home dividends. Of your $12.3 million wealth after 50 years, 95 percent is due to the home dividends.

What if the price of your home doesn't go up at all during the next 30 years? This is a wildly implausible scenario, but Figure 3.3 demonstrates that your home can be a great investment even if home prices don't increase and you earn a conservative 5 percent return on the annual investment of your home dividends.

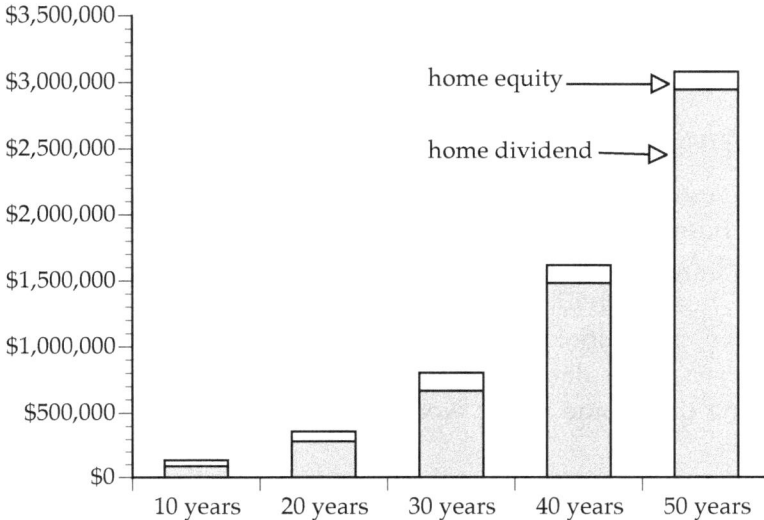

Figure 3.3 Your home is a great investment
even if home prices don't increase!

In this example, your home equity increases to $135,000 as your mortgage is paid off and then stays at $135,000 because of our unrealistic assumption that home prices never increase. Meanwhile, your home dividends are steadily building wealth. You will have a total wealth—home equity plus home dividends —of $800,000 after 30 years, $1.6 million after 40 years, and $3.1 million after 50 years. If you invest the home dividends at 10 percent, you will have $1.6 million after 30 years, $4.4 million after 40 years, and $11.8 million after 50 years.

We need to say this one more time because this is one of the most important messages in this book and because so few people understand why their home is such a great investment. Some people say that a home is not a good investment because home prices historically have not gone up as much as stock prices. They are missing the point. Most of the financial benefits from home ownership come from the home dividends, not from price appreciation. Price appreciation can certainly be an added bonus, but that isn't the most persuasive reason for buying a home. Don't buy a home because you think the price will be 10 percent higher a year from now. Do buy a home because you think that in the long run, it is better to pay off a mortgage than to pay a landlord.

The Lynch's Southern California Home

The investment value of a home is critically dependent on the size of the home dividend. The house in Fishers is a cash cow because of the large home dividends. In different places and at different times, home dividends might be higher or smaller or even negative. Let's look at a home in Southern California in 2003, which is a particularly interesting time because many people were warning that home prices were too high in 2003 and would soon collapse.

Peter and Monica Lynch had rented for several years but were thinking about buying. They found a nice single-family house that the owner offered to rent for $1,900 a month or sell for $455,000. Home prices had increased quite a bit in 2001 and 2002 and the Lynches had read stories describing the real estate market as a bubble. They debated whether they should put off buying until home prices came back down. In retrospect, they should have bought a few years earlier, but that option was no longer available. The question on the table in 2003 was whether the home they were considering was a fundamentally sound investment— not because its price would rise rapidly, but because the home dividends justify the price.

If you try to time the stock market by guessing the best moment to buy and the best time to sell, you will almost certainly fail. The same is true of real estate prices. Instead of trying to guess home prices a week from now or a year from now, try to assess whether current home prices are high or low relative to the home dividends.

The Lynches estimated the rent savings, mortgage payment, property taxes, insurance, maintenance and so on— all the financial costs and benefits of homeownership. Table 3.2 shows their first-year home dividend.

Once again, the biggest financial benefit is the rent savings and the biggest expense is the mortgage. Because the Lynches could rent this home for $1,900 a month, their rent saving the first year is

12 × $1,900) = $22,800. At that time, the Lynches could get a 30-year mortgage with a 5.2 percent interest rate. With a 20 percent down payment, their annual mortgage payments would be $23,985.

Table 3.2 Home Dividend for a Southern California Home

Income and Expenses	Dollar Amount
Rent savings	$22,800
Mortgage payment	–$23,983
Property tax	–$5,005
Tax savings	$10,917
Insurance	–$412
Utilities	$0
Maintenance	–$4,550
Home dividend	–$235

Unlike the Fishers example, the mortgage payments are initially larger than the rent savings. When the other costs and benefits are taken into account, the first-year home dividend is negative. This is worrisome, but not necessarily fatal. Mortgage payments are the main cost of homeownership and, with a fixed rate mortgage, these will be constant for 30 years and then stop completely. The main benefit of homeownership is the rent savings and rents will increase relentlessly, year after year. If the rent increases by 3 percent a year (roughly the rate of inflation), the Lynch's home dividend turns positive in the second year. After 30 years, the mortgage payments will stop while the annual rent savings are $53,730 and still growing by 3 percent a year. That's why buying a home can be a sound investment. Your mortgage payments are fixed and then stop; your rent savings grow and never stop growing.

The Lynches assumed a 5 percent return on home dividend. They also made the conservative assumption that their home's price wouldn't be any higher 30, 40, or 50 years after they bought their home.

Figure 3.4 shows the growth of the accumulated home dividends and home equity over time with these cautious assumptions. Their home is still an attractive investment! After 30 years, their mortgage payments will have paid off their mortgage and given them $455,000 in home equity, even if the market price of their home hasn't increased at all. Meanwhile, their invested home dividends will have grown to almost $400,000, giving them a total wealth of more than $800,000. Their 20 percent down payment was $91,000. Having this $91,000 investment grow to $800,000 represents a 7.6 percent annual after-tax rate of return on their investment. If the market price of their home increases or they earn more than 5 percent on their home dividend investments, the Lynches will do even better.

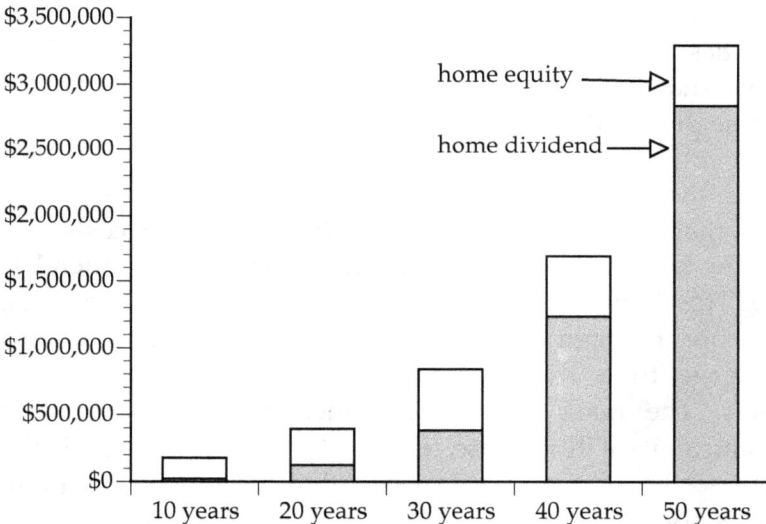

Figure 3.4 A home can be a great investment even if the first-year home dividend is negative

The Lynches were delighted with a 7.6 percent after-tax return because this was much better than they were doing with their other investments. Despite the Lynch's reservations about the recent run-up in home prices, this house appeared to be worth buying for $455,000.

They decided to buy. Three years later, they estimated the market price of their home to be $850,000. Then price fell over the next five years to $550,000 and rebounded to $750,000 in 2015.

Whee! They were certainly delighted that they bought this home for $455,000, but it would have been a profitable long-term investment even if the price had not fluctuated at all.

Your Home Is Not an ATM

Bill and Bette Andrews bought a house in Ohio in 1996 for $140,000. Ten years later, in 2006, they sold their house for $230,000. If they had left well enough alone, the $90,000 price increase would have been a nice bonus in addition to their annual home dividends and all the pleasure they derived from living in a home of their own for ten years.

Unfortunately, they didn't leave well enough alone. They did not invest their home dividends. Instead, they were serial borrowers. They spent the money they saved by not paying rent on frivolities. And as the value of their house increased, they took out home equity loans. Every time the value of their house increased by $10,000, they borrowed $10,000 (and sometimes more than $10,000). By the time they sold their house in 2006, they had outstanding loans of more than $225,000. In fact, the reason they sold their house is that they could no longer make the monthly payments on all their debts. By the time they sold their house, they didn't even have enough money left to pay the realtor's commission.

This story might not be so disheartening if the Andrews had used their home dividends and home equity loans to pay for important things like their children's college expenses. But they didn't have any children and they didn't use their home dividends and loans to buy anything particularly useful, let alone essential. They bought cars, boats, vacations, and other status symbols that they could have and should have done without.

A home is not an ATM. A home is a wonderfully rewarding and gratifying way to put a roof over your head and build your wealth. It should not be used to squander money on things you don't need and can't afford.

The Millionaire Paupers

Anna and Michael McCarthy bought a home in Connecticut for $250,000 in 1996. They made a $50,000 down payment and borrowed $200,000 at a 7 percent interest rate. Even though they both worked full time, they worried because they didn't save much. Their salaries were increasing, but they soon had two children and a family of four has a lot of expenses, including day care. They both had good jobs in 2005, but they could barely make ends meet: they didn't own any stocks, didn't have much money in the bank, and had $10,000 in credit-card debt. They said their finances "are a mess" and they argued about whose fault it was.

The reality is that they were actually pretty wealthy in 2005. Their home dividends paid for day care, their house had a market value of about $650,000, and their mortgage payments reduced their mortgage balance to $170,000. If they were to sell their home, they would walk away with $480,000 in cash (less the expenses involved in the sale):

Home sale price	$650,000
Mortgage balance	−$170,000
Equity	$480,000

Anna and Michael also had more than $300,000 in the retirement plans where they work. Their net worth was approximately $800,000! Anna and Michael were almost millionaires and they didn't even realize it.

Anna and Michael should try to accumulate some wealth outside their home and their retirement plans, and this got easier for them when their children entered public schools and Anna and Michael could invest their home dividends instead of spending the dividends on day care. They should also refinance their home mortgage in order to get a lower interest rate and pay off their credit-card debt, but that's another story.

Homes North, South, East, and West

In 2005, we looked at hundreds of single-family homes in the ten areas of the country shown in Table 3.3. In all ten areas, we estimated the home dividends by matching houses that had recently been sold with nearby houses that had recently been rented.

In every city, the average house we looked at was roughly a 3-bedroom, 2-bath, 1800-square-foot home. Each of our matched pairs was very similar in size, as well as being geographically pretty close to each other. We had good comps. The difference between our comps and the comps used by realtors is that we compared buying with renting, while they compare buying with buying.

Table 3.3 shows the estimated after-tax rate of return over infinite horizons for the average home in all ten areas. These calculations assume that rents increase, on average, by 3 percent a year.

Table 3.3 Average Implicit After-Tax Returns

Cities	Percent
San Mateo, CA	4.6
Orange County, CA	5.9
Los Angeles, CA	6.6
Boston, MA	6.7
Chicago, IL	7.2
San Bernardino, CA	7.3
New Orleans, LA	13.0
Dallas, TX	13.0
Atlanta, GA	18.4
Indianapolis, IN	21.2

New Orleans, Dallas, Atlanta, and Indianapolis all have double-digit returns. If you would be happy with a 10 percent after-tax return (who wouldn't?), then homes in these four areas were attractively priced. People who bought homes in the Heartland in 2005 are likely to find their homes to be a remarkably profitable investment in the long run. (Remember, too, that these calculations underestimate the value of homes to the extent that home buyers value privacy and other non-financial factors.)

At the other end of the spectrum, San Mateo home prices seem high unless you are satisfied with a low return or are a speculator who is counting on home prices to increase rapidly. In the other five areas (Orange County, Boston, Los Angeles, San Bernardino, and Chicago) homes were reasonably attractive investments in 2005, though surely not as attractive as they were a few years earlier.

Housing prices had increased rapidly in many areas by 2005 and some home buyers had unrealistic expectations about future prices. The relevant question, however, is not how much prices had increased in the past or how fast they might increase in the future, but whether, at current prices, a home is still a fundamentally sound investment. Our answer in 2005 was generally yes. Your answer today will depend on the particular home you are considering.

Table 3.4 shows the average increase in home prices in these ten areas in the ten years following our 2005 analysis. The top two performers (Dallas and New Orleans) were among the four areas with projected double-digit implicit returns in the long run. The third area (Indianapolis) also did relatively well, while the fourth (Atlanta) had a slight decrease in home prices.

Table 3.4 Average Increase in Home Prices, 2005 – 2015

Cities	Percent
Dallas, TX	32.7
New Orleans, LA	20.6
San Mateo, CA	20.1
Indianapolis, IN	6.0
Los Angeles, CA	3.6
Orange County, CA	0.5
Atlanta, GA	−0.4
Boston, MA	−3.8
Chicago, IL	−10.9
San Bernardino, CA	−14.6

Remember, however, that the long-run implicit returns calculated in 2005 did not rely on home prices increasing. Nonetheless. Figure 3.5 shows that areas with high implicit returns in 2005 tended to have relatively strong prices over the next decade. The exception is San Mateo, whose high prices in 2005 were even higher in 2015, perhaps because the enormous demand for housing in the Silicon Valley pushed up rents as well as prices.

Price Change 2005 - 2015, percent

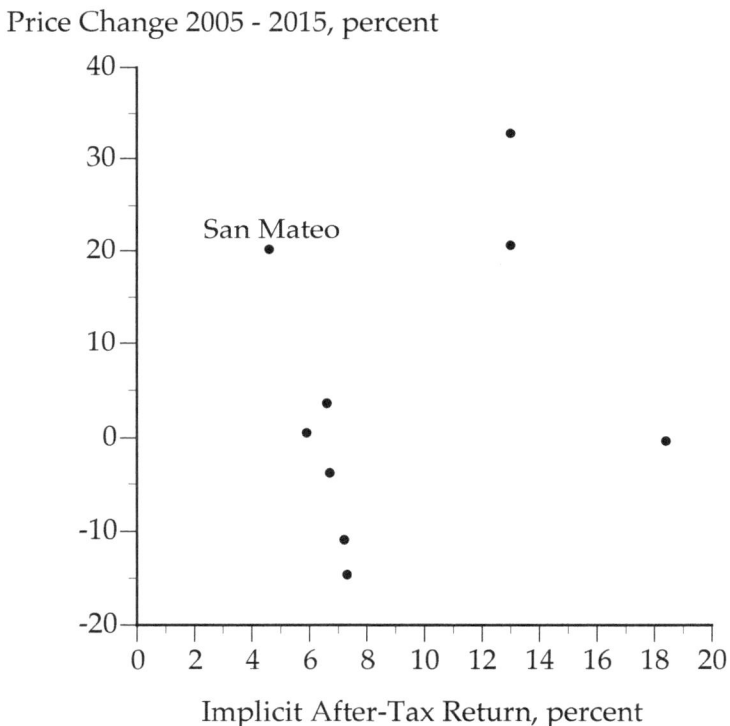

Implicit After-Tax Return, percent

Figure 3.5 The most attractively priced homes in 2005
did relatively well over the next 10 years

All real estate is local. We've shown you our conclusions for the average home in ten different regions in order to show you how the results can be quite different in different parts of the country. The only way to gauge whether your home or a home you are thinking about buying is likely to be a good investment is to estimate the home dividends. Appendix C, "Your Home," will help you do this.

The Bottom Line

1. People who fixate on price appreciation—believing that the only way to make money in real estate is if prices go up by 10 percent a year—miss the whole point about investing in a home. The home dividend is the cash cow that makes a home a great investment.
2. The home dividend increases over time because the main benefit (the rent savings) is growing while the main expense (the mortgage payment) is not.
3. Because of the high costs of buying and selling, buying a home is more likely to be profitable if you live in your home for several years.
4. Don't buy a home because you think the price will be 10 percent higher a year from now. Do buy a home because you think that in the long run your home dividends will make your home a great investment. Plus it is a lot more satisfying to own the home you live in than to own a bunch of rent receipts.
5. Your home is an investment; don't use it as an ATM. Don't squander your home dividends on junk. Don't use home equity loans to buy things you don't need.
6. In most of the United States, homes are an attractive investment.

4

Finding a Home and Closing the Deal

You're thinking seriously about buying a home. How, exactly, do you buy a home? It is certainly more complicated than going to the grocery store, but it is a lot more fun than buying a car. If you have never bought a home before, the process can seem intimidating. You have to learn a new language and sign an avalanche of papers. Don't be intimidated. There is a well-defined sequence of steps. The new language is straightforward and the paperwork is mostly designed to protect everyone involved. Millions of people have bought homes and you can, too.

Your first task is to determine the mortgage payments you can afford, because this will determine how much money you can borrow and, therefore, how much you can afford to pay for a home. Then you need to decide whether you want to use a realtor and, with or without one, find a home you want in your price range. Then come the negotiations that will close the deal.

How Much Home Can You Afford?

No matter whether you own or rent, it is imprudent to spend too much of your income on housing. If you do, you will have little money left for food, clothing, entertainment and all the other things that make life enjoyable. A conventional rule of thumb is that housing expenses shouldn't be more than 30 percent to 40 percent of a household's total income before taxes have been deducted.

Table 4.1 shows how these guidelines work. If your annual income is $50,000, then you can reasonably afford to pay between $1,250 and $1,667 a month for housing.

Table 4.1 Monthly Payments on a 30-Year Mortgage

Before-Tax Income		Monthly Housing Expenses	
Annual	*Monthly*	*30% of Income*	*40% of Income*
$20,000	$1,667	$500	$667
$30,000	$2,500	$750	$1,000
$40,000	$3,333	$1,000	$1,333
$50,000	$4,176	$1,250	$1,667
$60,000	$5,000	$1,500	$2,000
$70,000	$5,833	$1,750	$2,333
$80,000	$6,667	$2,000	$2,667
$90,000	$7,500	$2,250	$3,000
$100,000	$8,333	$2,500	$3,333
$120,000	$10,000	$3,000	$4,000
$140,000	$11,667	$3,500	$4,667
$160,000	$13,333	$4,000	$5,333
$180,000	$15,000	$4,500	$6,000
$200,000	$16,667	$5,000	$6,667

These are guidelines, not strict rules. You can afford to pay a bit more if you are buying than if you are renting because the interest on your mortgage is tax deductible, but rent payments are not. If you have other debts to pay (for example, car loans or spousal support), you can't afford to spend as much on housing. If your income is unstable or insecure (for example, most of your income is commission-based or you might be laid off), then you should be more cautious about your housing expenses. If you are confident that your income will increase substantially (for example, you are going to get promoted or your spouse is starting work), you might be able to afford higher housing expenses.

The first part of our affordability question is answered in Table 4.1: how much you can afford to pay each month. The second part is what those monthly payments will buy. If you are paying rent, this question is easy to answer. If your annual income is $50,000, Table 4.1 shows that you can afford to pay between $1,250 and $1,667 a month in rent. If you are buying a home, you will make mortgage payments instead of rent payments, and mortgage payments depend on interest rates.

Table 4.2 shows illustrative numbers. At a 6 percent interest rate, for example, the monthly payments on a $200,000 mortgage are $1,199. If you have $50,000 for a down payment, you can borrow $200,000, buy a $250,000 home, and have monthly payments of $1,199. That's your bottom line: If you can afford monthly mortgage payments of $1,199, you can afford to buy a $250,000 home.

Table 4.2 Monthly Payments on a 30-Year Mortgage

		Interest Rate		
Mortgage	4%	5%	6%	7%	8%
$50,000	$239	$268	$300	$333	$367
$100,000	$477	$537	$600	$665	$734
$200,000	$955	$1,074	$1,199	$1,331	$1,468
$300,000	$1,432	$1,610	$1,799	$1,996	$2,201
$400,000	$1,910	$2,147	$2,398	$2,661	$2,935
$500,000	$2,387	$2,684	$2,998	$3,327	$3,669
$600,000	$2,864	$3,221	$3,597	$3,992	$4,403
$700,000	$3,342	$3,758	$4,197	$4,657	$5,136
$800,000	$3,819	$4,295	$4,796	$5,322	$5,870

When you are figuring out how much you can afford to spend on housing, you should also include your estimated monthly payments for property taxes and homeowner's insurance; suppose that for the homes you are looking at in your area, monthly property taxes will be around $200 and monthly insurances will be about $80:

Mortgage payment	$1,199
Property taxes	$200
Homeowner's insurance	$80
Total monthly housing expense	$1,479

If your annual income is $50,000, then your housing expense of $1,479 is well within your range of $1,250 to $1,667.

Calculations like those in Table 4.2 also show how important mortgage rates are for home affordability. Let's keep the monthly payments at $1,199 and see how big a loan you would get if the mortgage rate was 4 percent or 8 percent, instead of 6 percent. Although the numbers aren't shown in Table 4.2, you can afford to borrow $251,000 if the mortgage rate is 4 percent, but can only borrow $163,000 if the mortgage rate is 8 percent. That's an $88,000 swing—the difference between being able to buy a $213,000 home and a $301,000 home.

If you can't afford your dream home, that's okay. Dreams are your goals, your aspirations—what you aim for. Buying a small home you can afford is usually better than waiting years while you try to save enough to buy your dream home. If you start small, you can invest your home dividends and build up equity until you are ready to trade up to your dream. If you wait to buy, home prices might go up as fast as your income (or even faster) and you might never be able to afford your dream home.

How to Choose a Home

Some people like old homes, some like new homes. Some like big yards, some think a yard is a nuisance. Some want to live close to schools, some don't want to be near noisy children. The choice is up to you.

The three most important things in real estate are location, location, location. So, start by identifying your ideal location. Think about your commute to work, the neighborhood schools, shopping, or whatever matters to you. After you identify your ideal location, see if you can afford a home there. If you can't, then consider the next best location.

A good house in a great location is much better than a great house in a bad location. By bad location, we don't just mean a crime-infested neighborhood. A home that is two hours from work is a bad location. A home in a flood plain is a bad location. A home in an airport flight path is a bad location. Anything that irritates you makes for a bad location. If you buy a home in a bad location, you are going to regret it until you move to a good location. So, why not start in a good location?

Realtors and newspaper advertisements have traditionally been the main sources of information about homes that are for sale. You can't tell much about a home from an ad in the newspaper, but newspapers are a good way to find out about open houses, which is when you can see what a home is really like. Go to several open houses and see what homes are in your price range look like. Make a list of what you like and dislike about each home. This list will help you remember the homes, which will become a blur after several open houses. More importantly, your list will help you identify what you are looking for in a home. If you go to an open house and don't like it because the low ceilings make it feel cramped, you now know that high ceilings are important to you. If you like a open house because it has a 3-car garage, you now know that this is important to you.

You can also use your own newspaper ads to help you find a home. When Steve and Linda Cox were moving to Texas, they put a small ad in a local newspaper stating that they were looking to buy a home in a certain area in a specified price range. They received six replies: two from realtors and four from homeowners who hadn't yet put their homes on the market. Steve and Linda looked at several homes, including the four that weren't yet on the market. They ended up buying one.

Real estate brokers are also a useful source of information because they have access to a local multiple listing service (MLS) where realtors share information with each other about properties that are on the market or have sold recently. When you use a realtor to help you sell your home, the realtor typically puts the home in the MLS database as a kind of advertisement, hoping to persuade other realtors to show the home to potential buyers. The MLS listing usually shows a picture of the home and the property's address, square footage, number of bedrooms and bathrooms, and other details. The listing agent's comments are also included, such as CUTE AS A BUTTON! GREAT STARTER HOME! DON'T MISS THIS DOLLHOUSE! (In real estate lingo, these are all euphemisms for small.) MLS descriptions are often in capital letters with lots of exclamation points because the listing realtor is trying to catch the attention of other realtors.

The listing realtor might hold an open house for realtors, usually on a weekday, as part of a realtor caravan. The caravan starts at a designated time and place, and travels to a sequence of homes that are new to the market. The caravan stops at each home, and the realtors are in and out in a few minutes and off to the next home. The idea is to get a feel for what each home is really like so that the realtors can better match homes and buyers.

How to Choose a Realtor

How do you choose a realtor? A good starting point is to ask yourself what you want your realtor to do for you. If you are buying a home, a list of realtor chores might look like this:

1. Screen homes
2. Negotiate a reasonable price
3. Handle the paperwork

Handling the paperwork is important, but this is not going to narrow your realtor choices very much. If your realtor is an experienced and licensed professional working for a good firm, the paperwork is mostly straightforward. You will have to make decisions about a few things (for example, how much time the other side has to respond to your offer), but good realtors will guide you to reasonable choices.

The same is true of price negotiations. All the good realtors in your area will look at the same comps and come up with a similar range of prices. Ultimately, you decide how much to offer for a home, and you should pay more attention to the home dividends than to the realtor. If you really want the home and it is well worth the price, then go for it. Otherwise, see if you can get a better price.

The most important realtor task might be screening homes for you. If you are a busy person, few things are as frustrating as driving around to look at homes that you would never consider living in. A good realtor will quickly figure out what appeals to you. After all, realtors don't want to waste their time either. A good realtor will know how much house you can afford, what neighborhoods you like, how big a house you want, what style you like, and so on. If you know what you want, then a good realtor will know what you want.

A good realtor is a good listener and knows the homes on the market so that buyers and homes can be matched. Think of a good realtor as a matchmaker, and then you will know what to look for in a realtor.

Scott and Emily Cho went to San Clemente, California, for a day at the beach. After lunch at a local restaurant, they decided to stop by a local realtor's office. A friendly realtor greeted them, and Scott and Emily told her that they might be interested in buying a vacation home. The realtor said, "Let me see what's available," and started searching through MLS listings. This realtor didn't know what was on the market and didn't ask Scott and Emily about the kind of home they might like. She was not a good matchmaker. Scott and Emily thanked the realtor for her time and headed for the beach.

The starting point for finding a good realtor is recommendations from people you trust. Don't judge a realtor by ads in the newspaper. Some of the best realtors don't advertise because they have plenty of word-of-mouth referrals. They might not even hold open houses. Mary Lou Bolton, for example, is a very successful realtor who doesn't hold open houses because she doesn't want to a waste day showing homes mostly to curious neighbors (what realtors call *looky loos*) and she doesn't want to worry about damage or theft at her clients' homes. She only shows homes to people who are serious about buying and who she thinks are the right fit for the home. She doesn't advertise in the paper because she doesn't need to and because she doesn't want to burn hours with people who aren't serious buyers or sellers. And yet she is consistently one of the top three agents in her town because she attracts serious clients and focuses her energies on matching people and homes.

Is the Price Right?

One type of information provided by realtors is comps, the selling prices (or asking prices for houses that haven't yet sold) of comparable properties that are close by with similar square footage. Realtors get these comps from their MLS databases. The most successful realtors also know the pluses and minuses of each property. "That home is very dark. That home has just been totally remodeled by the best contractor in town. That home is in an airport flight path." This intimate knowledge can help you narrow your search quickly and efficiently, and also help you put together truly accurate comps.

A property's list price is the seller's asking price. The negotiated sale price is usually somewhat less than the list price, and sometimes considerably lower, depending on how realistic the list price is. In hot markets, buyers sometimes get into bidding wars and end up paying more than the list price. A potentially telling bit of information is how long the home has been on the market. Homes that have been on the market a long time are probably priced too high and the owners might be willing to accept a substantially lower price.

This House Will Be Sold on November 11

We were visiting relatives in Menlo Park, California, in 1999 and noticed an open house around the corner. We weren't serious buyers, just looky loos. And what we saw was very interesting! The house itself was problematic: a long, single-story L-shape with no hallways so we had to walk through rooms in order to get to other rooms. One of the "bedrooms" was at the bend in the L, with the bed at an odd angle and no windows. We had to walk through this bedroom to get from one side of the house to the other side.

But everything looked tremendous because the house had been professionally staged. Stagers are hired to make a house as appealing as possible. The simplest staging involves cleaning up and organizing what is already there, and adding a few decorative touches like monogrammed towels and flower vases. More elaborate staging involves replacing dated furniture, worn rugs, and boring pictures with more fashionable furnishings. This home was so stunningly decorated that it almost (but not quite) made us overlook the bizarre floor plan.

One of the most interesting things about this open house was that the flyer for the property said that the asking price was $1.1 million and that the owners would accept offers for the next 10 days, until November 11, at which point the house would be sold to the highest offer. In cool markets, having one open house and thinking that the house will sell in 10 days is presumptuous. But this was a hot market. The sellers were confident that they would receive multiple offers, many above the asking price. By setting a 10-day deadline for offers and not revealing the offers, they hoped to persuade nervous buyers to bid high. This house sold on November 11, for $1.26 million.

The 6 Percent Fortress

The Internet is great. You can use the Internet to find clear instructions for fixing a leaky faucet, accurate directions to a birthday party, and the e-mail addresses of long-lost friends. One of the most powerful, truly revolutionary features of the Internet is that it helps buyers and sellers find each other and makes it easy to compare prices. You aren't going to pay $20 for a can of Illy coffee at a local store if you can buy it online for $11. If enough people feel the same way, local stores will have to offer competitive prices. The same is true of bookstores, toy stores, computer stores, and travel agents. Businesses have a much harder time charging high prices if customers have the option of buying low-priced products on the Internet.

The Internet has even affected the prices of cars and other large items that cannot be easily mailed. In the old days, about the only way to buy a car was to go to a car dealer and haggle for hours, with little or no idea of whether the price the dealer offered was higher or lower than the price that you might be able to negotiate with another dealer. To find that out, you had to go to other dealers and haggle some more. Nowadays, the Internet can rescue you from interminable haggling. You can use the Internet to get price quotations from several dealers for a specific car and either buy from one of these dealers or use their quotes as the basis for streamlined negotiating: "I can buy this car for $24,350; if you can beat this price, I will buy it from you." The Internet helps you become an informed shopper. It can also dramatically reduce the cost of buying a car—not only the final price but also the hours wasted with car dealers. Many of us would rather have a colonoscopy than argue with a car dealer.

The Internet has the potential to offer the same benefits to home buyers that it offers to car buyers, but that potential has not yet been fully realized. Traditionally, you shop for a home by using a realtor who has access to the local MLS. The realtor uses the MLS to find homes that might appeal to you and then shows you the ones that interest you. When you find a home you like, the realtor uses the MLS to show you the prices of comparable homes that have recently sold.

The cost? Traditionally, the seller pays a commission equal to 6 percent of the sale price, with the commission split equally between the seller's agent and the buyer's agent. If the agent works for a real estate company (as most do), the 3 percent commission is divided between the company and the agent. If there is a 50-50 split, then the agent ends up with a commission equal to 1.5 percent of the sale price. Superstar agents are often able to negotiate splits that are 70-30, 80-20, 90-10, or even 95-5. The owner of a Las Vegas real estate office told us that she has a 95-5 split with her star agent because he would leave otherwise, and she would rather get 5 percent of $1 million than 50 percent of nothing.

You don't have to use a realtor to buy or sell a house, but most people do because good realtors have an intimate knowledge of the local market and valuable experience in handling the paperwork involved in a real estate transaction. Still, a 6 percent commission is very high. A 6 percent commission is $18,000 on a $300,000 home, $30,000 on a $500,000 home, and $60,000 on a million-dollar home. In the age of the Internet, there is no compelling economic reason why a realtor should cost so high. If the homes that are for sale were described fully on the Internet, most buyers are perfectly capable of finding ones worth seeing. If recent home sales in a specific area were described fully on the Internet, most buyers are perfectly capable of comparing prices.

The one thing that realtors can do better than most homebuyers is handle the paperwork that accompanies real estate transactions (though, frankly, a lot of the paperwork just protects the realtor from being sued). Even so, the paperwork is not worth the tens of thousands of dollars you pay for a realtor's commission.

So why do realtors charge a 6 percent commission? Because they can.

Our advice? If you are buying a home, go with an experienced realtor who is a great matchmaker. If you are selling a home, go with an experienced realtor who will give you a break on the commission.

Moving Merchandise

Realtors say that their negotiating skills are invaluable, that they earn their commission by getting the best price for their clients. However, buyers, sellers, and realtors have somewhat different goals. The buyer wants a low price and the seller wants a high price; the agent wants to close the deal and move on to the next house. Stores make money by moving merchandise. Realtors make money by moving houses.

Suppose for example, that a home is listed for $420,000, with a 6 percent realtor's commission. If the house is sold for $400,000, each realtor will get a $12,000 commission (some of which goes to their firms). If the seller's agent can get the price up to $410,000, that's an extra $10,000 for the seller, but only an extra $300 for the realtor. If the buyer's agent can get the price down to $390,000, the buyer saves $10,000, but the realtor loses $300.

The buyer and seller are keenly interested in getting the best possible price. But $300 is nothing to a realtor compared to the $12,000 commission that might be lost if the deal isn't done. If there is no sale, the seller's agent has to keep marketing the property, holding open houses, and talking with the seller—and the house might not sell for months. The buyer's agent has to keep showing houses and talking with the buyer—and the buyer might end up buying nothing at all.

Both realtors want very much to close the deal. That is why some realtors are more inclined to persuade their clients to accept the other side's offer than to jeopardize the deal by trying to negotiate a better price.

Herb Jones once sold one house and bought another house in the same western Massachusetts city at the same time, using the same realtor. When Herb was negotiating the selling price, the realtor told him that the real estate market was cooling and that he should accept a lower price than suggested by the comps. When Herb was negotiating the purchase price, the realtor told him that the real estate market was hot and that he should pay a higher price than suggested by the comps! The realtor wanted to move the merchandise.

You might think that the buyer's realtor wants to negotiate the lowest price. Nope. Most realtors think their job is to "sell the home" because they don't make a penny unless the home is sold. Their incentive is to persuade buyers that it is a great home at a great price. Buyers are naturally wary of the seller's agent, but they should be a wary of their own agent as well. Listen carefully when your realtor shows you a home. "Oh, what a lovely view! I love these high ceilings. Solid wood floors are under the carpet. This is a great stove." Every little remark is intended to nudge you into buying.

Sometimes sellers pay buyers' agents extra bonuses on top of the usual commission. In such cases, there is a clear conflict of interest. Will the buyer's agent treat all homes equally or focus on those homes with the biggest payoff? Even worse, sellers sometimes make the bonus contingent on the buyer paying the full asking price. Agents who are looking out for their clients will try to get the best price. Agents who are looking out for themselves will try to get the largest commission.

After you buy a home, your agent will send you a basket of goodies and congratulate you on your great purchase. "I can't believe what a great deal you got on this lovely home. I would have bought it myself if I had the money." Lawyers say that regardless of whether they win or lose a case, what matters most is that their clients are happy to pay the bill. It's the same with realtors.

Happy Clients

John Logan had an enlightening courtroom experience. John was involved in a civil case and both parties hired prominent, expensive lawyers. There was a pretrial meeting of the lawyers and clients in a private room at the courthouse, and the two lawyers went at it tooth-and-nail, arguing, name-calling, table-banging. Clearly, each lawyer was going all out for their clients, and neither would back down. Then the lawyers met with the judge in his chambers, while the clients waited outside. When the lawyers returned, they said that the judge had told them off the record what the likely outcome of a trial would be and suggested a settlement consistent with that outcome. Both lawyers started in again, this time directing much of their fury toward the judge for not fully appreciating their side of the case. The clients were satisfied that their lawyers had done the best they could and there seemed no point in paying for an expensive trial. They agreed to the settlement that had reportedly been suggested by the judge.

John was almost out of the courthouse when he realized that he had left his pen in the private room. As he approached the room, he heard the lawyers laughing and congratulating each other on the great show they had put on for their clients. Right then, John knew that it's not whether you win or lose, but whether the clients are happy to pay their legal bills.

The Closer

Bill James is a shark posing as a realtor, but other realtors say they love working with Bill because he closes deals. It doesn't matter whether Bill represents the buyer or seller. If the parties are serious, Bill sees to it that the deal gets done. In one case, Bill was representing both the buyer and seller (which is a bit dodgy) and was showing the home before other realtors knew it was for sale. The negotiations were stuck at a $417,500 offer by the buyer and a $420,000 counteroffer by the seller. After it became clear that neither side would budge, Bill told the sellers that if they accepted the $417,500 offer, he would reduce his commission by $2,500. Bill's deal with his agency is that he gets 90 percent of a 6 percent commission. On a \$417,500 transaction, that's \$22,545. He gave up \$2,500 to ensure that the deal would go through and he would net a little over \$20,000.

In another transaction, Bill was representing the buyer and a price had been agreed to, subject to a home inspection. After the inspection, the buyer came back with a long list of nuisance requests, including a leaky faucet and a loose doorknob. The seller's realtor told them to "ignore the list; Bill will take care of it." Bill would either persuade the buyer to drop the list or give them some money to cover the cost of the repairs. Sure enough, the deal went through.

The Times They Are a Changing

There are some signs of weakness in the 6 percent fortress. Traditionally, MLS databases are considered proprietary information that homeowners can access only through a realtor. In response to competitive pressures, the National Association of Realtors created the www.realtor.com Web site, which allows everyone access to some MLS information about properties that are for sale. Additionally, many local realtors have online lists of homes available in their area. If their clients pre-screen properties, the realtor has less work to do. And customers who use the Web site might follow up by contacting the realtor who posted the listing.

Much more jealously guarded is MLS information on actual sale prices. This information isn't useful for pre-screening properties and won't lead to new business. But it does give the realtor something valuable that it is difficult for customers to get on their own—the comps that are used to negotiate prices. Realtors have very good reasons for not giving this information away, so they don't.

Sellers can often negotiate lower commissions with realtors who prefer getting a 4 percent commission to getting nothing at all. Sellers' agents might agree to a 5 percent or 4 percent commission, or maybe a 5 percent commission with 3 percent to the seller's agent and 2 percent to the buyer's agent. Buyers' agents might agree to give part of their commission to the buyer.

Sellers' and buyers' agents might agree to use part of their commission to pay for various closing costs or minor repairs that need to be done to close the deal. Commissions are still high, but they are moving in the right direction.

Some of the pressure to change commissions comes from Internet brokers who give customers up to 75 percent of their commission. Unfortunately, some conventional brokers play hardball with online brokers by refusing to bring buyers to homes listed by online brokers and refusing to show homes to online buyers. Would realtors do this if they were really looking out for their customers? How do buyers benefit if realtors won't show them homes that might interest them? How do sellers benefit if realtors don't allow some buyers to see their homes?

Match This

Lucy and John Kim used a local realtor to show them homes in Miami. They found a million-dollar home they liked and were ready to make an offer. Lucy contacted an Internet broker and found out that she could get a $7,000 credit towards the purchase price. The broker would collect the normal 3 percent commission on the sale and give the Kims 25 percent of this commission ($7,000). Lucy wasn't completely comfortable using an Internet broker and she felt a little guilty about abandoning the local realtor who had taken the time to show them several homes. But she did like that $7,000 credit. So, Lucy phoned the local realtor and told her about the Internet broker and the $7,000 credit. The local realtor decided that 75 percent of the commission was better than nothing, and quickly agreed to give the Kims a $7,000 credit. The Kims bought the house and got their $7,000. The realtor got a reduced, but still substantial, commission. The Internet broker didn't get any money this time, but did put some healthy, competitive pressure on the 6 percent fortress.

Realtors: Can't Live With Them or Without Them

The Bensons were looking for a house close to their jobs and big enough for their growing family. One Saturday, Mrs. Benson noticed a tiny two-line advertisement in their local paper for an open house the next day from 1 to 4 o'clock in the afternoon. There was no description of the house, no price, and no phone number. Just the address.Could the owner not afford a bigger ad or was this a clever ploy to build interest through secrecy?

Sunday turned out to be miserably cold and rainy. The Bensons waited for a break in the rain, and it finally slowed to a cold drizzle around 3 o'clock. On the way to the house, they noticed that two realtor open houses had been canceled because of the bad weather. Maybe buyers were staying home to keep dry? Or maybe sellers didn't want people tracking mud into their homes.

When the Bensons got to the address given in the two-line ad, there was no for-sale sign in front. The mystery deepened! Did they have the wrong address? Mrs. Benson knocked on the door and found out that this was indeed the house with the two-line ad. It was for sale by ownerIt was for sale by owner and the wife was in the kitchen while the husband was in the garage. The Bensons signed a guest book with five other names in it. Not many people had seen the ad and ventured out in the rain.

The house itself was an interesting 80-year-old Craftsman that needed work. The upstairs had four bedrooms (one not much bigger than a closet and one with a sagging 7-foot ceiling) and one nonworking bathroom. But the house was two blocks from work, one block from the elementary school their children would attend, and had a double lot where their four children could play.

If the price was right, this was their dream house. But what was the price? The owners didn't have a price. They were apparently hoping for a bidding war and all they would say was, "Make us an offer."

The Bensons brought in Darlene, a local realtor with a winning personality who might help the sellers identify a fair price and close the deal. But Darlene's realty office wouldn't let her take a commission or side payment from the buyers; they only took commissions from sellers. So, the Bensons told Darlene that if they were able to buy this house, they would let Darlene sell their house with a full 6 percent commission. As it turned out, Darlene's personality won over the sellers, and they were intimidated by all the legal documents needed to sell a house. They agreed to pay Darlene a 2 percent commission to help them sell their home. Even a for-sale-by-owner may need a realtor.

Negotiating Boldly

Sometimes patience is best, sometimes a bold move works. Faced with sellers who wouldn't set a price, the Bensons made an initial low-ball offer to test the water. The seller immediately countered with a price that was 50 percent higher—a price that was clearly too high and left the buyer and seller far apart.

The Bensons figured that the sellers had not given an initial price because they were hoping for a bidding war. The Bensons also knew that not many people knew the house was for sale—no sign was in the front yard—but that news travels fast in their town and some aggressive realtors would try to list this property.

So the Bensons decided to make a bold move. With the help of the realtor, Darlene, they estimated a reasonable price for the house based on comps. They also estimated the home dividends and it looked like this house was an attractive investment. Finally, the Bensons knew that the seller had bought the house 20 years ago and would be happy with a large profit.

They asked Darlene to present the offer that evening, after the sellers had come home from work and finished dinner. Darlene would explain that the Bensons wanted to buy the house and that Darlene had looked at the comps and come up with a fair price. But the Bensons were not going to let their offer be used as a bargaining tool. Darlene would not leave the seller's house until the sellers had either signed the sale agreement or said no. The offer was take it or leave it—no counteroffers, no negotiating, no delaying.

Darlene would also point out that if the sellers did not sell the house privately, they would need a realtor who would want a 6 percent commission. Darlene was happy to make this offer because she believed that the price was fair and she wanted to close the deal. The Bensons were hoping that the sellers would choose certainty over uncertainty. Darlene presented the offer and went into the kitchen while the sellers talked it over. After about 30 minutes, the sellers accepted the offer.

Good Things Come to Those Who Wait

Sometimes patience is a virtue. The Garcias had saved enough money for a down payment and wanted to buy a house in Dallas. Home prices had peaked recently and were falling slightly. The Garcias wanted a relatively new tract home and dozens of possibilities were on the market. But most sellers were unwilling to accept the reality that a hot market had turned into a buyer's market.

The Garcias decided that patience was the best strategy. They didn't have a deadline for buying a house and it might take a while for sellers to accept the new reality. Plenty of acceptable houses were on the market and if the Garcias didn't get the first, second, or tenth house they made an offer on, they knew plenty more were available. So they made a series of offers 20 percent below what they were willing to pay. Each offer expired in 48 hours and if the responses weren't encouraging, the Garcias moved on to the next house. After a few months, they got a good house at a great price.

Regression to the Mean

A statistical expert once wrote that

> *There are few statistical facts more interesting than regression to the mean for two reasons. First, people encounter it almost every day of their lives. Second, almost nobody understands it. The coupling of these two reasons makes regression to the mean one of the most fundamental sources of error in human judgment.*

The general principle is that things that appear to be far above or below average probably are above or below average, but not as far from average as they seem. One example that resonates with most people is the search for partners. We don't know what you find attractive; so we will call it "pizzazz." You might be at work or play when you see someone who seems to have pizzazz. But when you get to know this person better, there is usually some disappointment. Regression to the mean! It is possible, but unlikely, that people who seem to have great pizzazz are actually better than they seem, but how many people, on an off day, would be the most attractive person in the room? This does not mean that we shouldn't choose those who appear to be the best. What it does mean is that we should be prepared for the likelihood that they are not as great as they initially appear to be.

This principle applies to many aspects of the real estate market. The house you love at first sight is probably not as good as it seems. It probably isn't a bad house; it just has a few warts you didn't notice the first time. If you are psychologically prepared for your dream home's regression to the mean, you won't panic or feel depressed when you discover the warts.

The same argument applies to the house's location. If you fall in love with the city and the neighborhood at first glance, you will probably be a little less thrilled after the second and third glances. This doesn't mean that you should not take second and third glances. You most certainly should! Regression to the mean teaches you that the city and neighborhood you think are perfect probably aren't flawless. You need to look again so that you can identify the imperfections.

Similarly, the realtor you choose probably isn't perfect. The contractor you choose for your remodeling job probably isn't perfect. The gardeners you choose probably aren't perfect. The neighbors who seem to have the most in common with you probably aren't perfect. One more time: This doesn't mean that you shouldn't choose what seems best, only that you should prepare yourself for the likelihood that many things are not as good as they initially seem.

Voltaire once said that the perfect is the enemy of the good. This means that if you demand perfection, you will be paralyzed by the hopelessness of this goal. You won't submit a report until it is perfect. You won't paint your house until you find the perfect color. You won't marry until you find the perfect spouse.

Regression to the mean is also why the grass is always greener on the other side of the fence. Don't give up what you have because what you covet is probably not as good as it seems. Don't sell your house three months after you buy it because you find a leaky faucet. Don't fire your realtor because you don't like the color of her car. Don't give up on your neighbors because they don't laugh at all your jokes. Don't divorce the spouse who sometimes forgets to put the cap back on the toothpaste. Nobody's perfect. Not even you!

Be satisfied with the good.

The Bottom Line

1. Estimate the home you can afford based on your income and current mortgage rates; be conservative.
2. When choosing a home, start with location. A good house in a great location is much better than a great house in a bad location.
3. You can identify the features you want in a home by going to several open houses and making a list of what you like and don't like about each home.
4. A good realtor is a good matchmaker who can narrow your choices quickly so that you don't waste time looking at homes that will disappoint you.
5. Market prices are heavily influenced by comps, but the range is often wide and you have room to negotiate, particularly in soft markets. If the home dividends are paltry, wait.
6. Don't let realtors pressure you into paying too much for a house.
7. The perfect is the enemy of the good. Don't be paralyzed by a hopeless search for perfection.

5

Debt Isn't Always a Four-Letter Word

Some people think debt is a four-letter word that well-behaved people should avoid: "If you can't pay cash, you can't afford it." Others think debt is the greatest invention ever: "Of course I can afford it. I'll just use my credit card." Both have a point. Too many people borrow too much money to buy things they really can't afford. On the other hand, borrowing money is what allows you to buy a home, which may well be the best purchase you will ever make.

In this chapter, we will explain two powerful financial principles:

1. Borrowing money is sometimes profitable.
2. Judging a loan by the total payments can be an expensive mistake.

You can apply these principles to several borrowing questions. If you can pay cash, does it make sense to take out a car loan? If you can afford to make a $50,000 down payment on a house, does it make sense to make a $30,000 down payment and keep $20,000 invested in stocks? If you can afford to pay off part of your mortgage early, should you do so? We begin with a discussion of the general principle that the investment of borrowed money can magnify the gains and losses from an investment. Then we will develop the framework for answering these questions and many more.

Using Loans to Live Beyond Your Means

Borrowed money creates wonderful opportunities to improve your life. If you couldn't borrow money to buy a home, few people would ever own homes. A mortgage allows you to make monthly mortgage payments instead of rent payments. After your mortgage is paid off, you own a valuable house instead of a worthless collection of rent receipts.

It is not just homes. Suppose you spend $40 a month to clean your clothes at a Laundromat because you can't afford to pay $1,000 for a washer and dryer. If you borrow $1,000 at a 10 percent interest rate to buy a washer and dryer, $40 a month will pay off the loan in 28 months. Then you don't have to keep spending $40 a month to clean your clothes at a laundromat. Plus, you don't have to spend hours traveling to the laundromat and reading old magazines about goofy celebrities while you wait for your clothes.

Unfortunately, the opportunity to buy things with borrowed money sometimes sucks people into buying things they don't really need—a luxury car, a 98-inch flat-screen plasma TV, designer clothes, time-share condominiums, snowmobiles, or jet skis. The real cost of borrowing money to buy extravagant things is that you could buy useful things if you didn't have these foolish debts to repay.

The first principle of borrowing is that loans are great for buying things you really need. Buying a washer and dryer can be less expensive than going to a laundromat. Buying a car can be less expensive than paying someone to drive you everywhere. Buying a home can be less expensive than renting one. You need to wash your clothes, go places, and live somewhere. The question is how to pay for these necessities. Borrowing money to buy a washer, car, and home may well be the answer.

On the other hand, loans also make it easy for us to live beyond our means. We don't need the most expensive washer, car, or house. A single person doesn't need to live in a 4,000-square-foot house; a family with two children doesn't need a home in Ohio and vacation homes on both coasts. We don't need a lot of diversions, dust-catchers, and other extravagances. Borrowing can be a necessity and also a temptation: a necessity when we need something like a home, but a temptation when we desire something we can live without.

How to Invest Like Warren Buffett

Gary bought his first home, a small 2-bedroom, 1-bath house in a modest neighborhood in Connecticut, for $28,000 in 1971. He was 26 years old and put $4,000 down and borrowed $24,000. Seven years later, he sold the house for $56,000, twice what he paid for it. This works out to an impressive, but not extraordinary, increase of 10.4 percent a year.

The monthly payments on a 30-year mortgage barely reduce the mortgage for the first several years and, indeed, Gary still owed the bank $22,000 when he sold this house in 1978. After repaying the mortgage, he walked away with a check for $34,000. A 100 percent increase in the value of the house increased the value of his investment by 750 percent, from $4,000 to $34,000! Gary's annualized rate of return was 35.8 percent. All Gary did was buy a rather ordinary house and he made 35.8 percent a year —better than Warren Buffett and other hotshots.

The point of this story is not that Gary is a better investor than Warren Buffett—he's not—but that borrowing money to buy a home can turn out to be an astonishingly profitable investment. Your secret weapon is leverage.

Loans Create Leverage

We have all seen news stories about people, perhaps even relatives or neighbors, who lost their home, farm, or business because they could not repay a loan. This is one reason why many people consider debt to be one of those four-letter words that decent people avoid. We have relatives who rented homes all their lives because they think it is imprudent to borrow money. It might even be dishonorable. A gentleman in Connecticut told us that everyone he knows pays cash for their homes because it is a sign of weakness to borrow money. No, I'm not kidding. On the other hand, some people swear by, not at, debt. Borrowing allows you to invest other people's money, and many a fortune has been built with other people's money.

Debt has two sides, a proverbial two-edged sword, because it creates leverage, in that a relatively small investment (your down payment) reaps the profits or losses from a much larger investment (your home). Suppose that you buy a home for $200,000 by making a $40,000 down payment and borrowing $160,000 at a 6 percent interest rate. You have 5-to-1 leverage because your $40,000 investment reaps the profits or losses from a home that is worth 5 times the size of your investment.

For simplicity, we will look a year into the future and assume that this is an interest-only loan. Table 5.1 shows some possible outcomes.

Table 5.1 Potential Returns on a $200,000 Home
with a $40,000 Down Payment

Return on $200,000 Home		Interest on $160,000 Mortgage	Return on $40,000 Down Payment	
Percent	Dollars	Dollars	Dollars	Percent
2	4,000	9,600	−5,600	−14
6	12,000	9,600	2,400	6
10	20,000	9,600	10,400	26
14	28,000	9,600	18,400	46

Look first at the case where the return on the home is 6 percent (the second row in Table 5.1). A 6 percent return on $200,000 is $12,000, enough to pay the interest due on the loan with $2,400 left over, which is a 6 percent return on the $40,000 your down payment. Not very exciting so far. But this illustrates the general principle that if you borrow at 6 percent in order to invest at 6 percent, then borrowing is neither an advantage nor a disadvantage.

What if the rate of return on the home turns out to be 10 percent? This time the profit is $10,400, which is a 26 percent return. Now we're talking. You earn 26 percent by borrowing at 6 percent and investing at 10 percent! Table 5.1 also shows that you will earn a remarkable 46 percent return if you borrow at 6 percent and invest at 14 percent.

The two-edged sword comes into play because leverage works on the downside, too, by multiplying shortfalls. If your home earns only a 2 percent return, your return is −14 percent. Your home made money but you lost money! Your total investment doesn't have to lose money for leverage to be a disaster; what hurts is that the investment's return is lower than the loan rate. You will lose money borrowing at 6 percent to invest at 2 percent.

The general principle is clear: Borrowing to invest is financially advantageous if the return on your investment is higher than the interest rate on your loan; otherwise, you may be in deep trouble. You will make money borrowing at 6 percent to invest at 10 percent; you will lose money borrowing at 6 percent to invest at 2 percent.

Leverage + Compounding = Wow!

Table 5.1 looks one year into the future. If we look several years ahead, compound interest makes leverage even more powerful. Suppose that you have a 6 percent, 30-year mortgage and that the annual return on your home (rent saving plus price appreciation, minus taxes and all expenses other than your mortgage) is 10 percent. Borrowing at 6 percent to invest at 10 percent is a winning combination. Let's see how that difference builds up over time.

Table 5.2 shows that after 5 years you will have a $67,986 profit on your initial $40,000 investment. After 30 years, you will have a $2,530,922 profit. Leverage is powerful and compounding is potent. Leverage plus compounding is amazing.

Table 5.2 Potential Return on a $200,000 Home

Year	Profit on $40,000 Down Payment	
	Dollars	*Percent*
1	10,400	26
5	67,986	170
10	192,213	481
20	792,358	1,981
30	2,530,922	6,327

Loan Payments

When you borrow money, you pay back what you borrowed plus interest. One kind of loan is an interest-only balloon loan, in which you pay interest on the loan until it matures and then pay back the entire amount you borrowed (the balloon payment). On some balloon loans, nothing—not even interest—is paid until the loan matures. In practice, most borrowers don't have enough money to make a balloon payment. That's why they borrowed in the first place! When their balloon loan matures, they need a new loan to pay off the old loan.

Before the Great Depression in the 1930s, most mortgages were 3-year to 5-year balloon loans. During the Great Depression, people who had lost their jobs couldn't make their mortgage payments. And banks didn't want to renew loans to people who might lose their jobs or had already lost them. Soon, people were losing not only their jobs but their homes, farms, and businesses.

After the Great Depression, short-term balloon loans were replaced with long-term (typically 30-year) mortgages that are amortized, which means that the monthly payments pay the interest that is due and also repay part of the amount borrowed. By the time the loan matures, the loan has been completely repaid. The most common amortized loan involves constant monthly payments over the life of the loan.

The Unpaid Balance

Table 5.3 shows some of the monthly details for a 30-year, $200,000 mortgage with a 6 percent interest rate and monthly payments of $1,199.10. With a 6 percent annual interest rate, the monthly interest rate is a half-percent.

After the first month, you owe a month's interest on your $200,000 debt, and a half-percent interest on $200,000 is $1,000. Your $1,199.10 monthly payment covers this interest and also reduces your mortgage by $199.10 (called your principal payment). Every month thereafter, you owe less interest because your unpaid balance is declining. Still, the monthly payments are mostly interest for the first several years and the loan is not half repaid until the twenty-first year. It takes 21 years to pay off half the loan and 9 years to pay off the remaining half.

Table 5.3 A 30-Year, $200,000 Amortized Loan at 6 Percent

Payment Number	Total Payment	Interest Payment	Principal Payment	Unpaid Balance
1	$1,199.10	$1000.00	$199.10	$199,800.90
2	$1,199.10	$999.00	$200.10	$199,600.80
3	$1,199.10	$998.00	$201.10	$199,399.70
60	$1,199.10	$931.88	$267.22	$186,108.80
120	$1,199.10	$838.66	$360.44	$167,371.60
240	$1,199.10	$543.32	$655.78	$108,007.66
300	$1,199.10	$314.55	$884.55	$62,024.89
359	$1,199.10	$6.00	$1,193.10	$1,193.13
360	$1,199.10	$5.97	$1,193.13	$0.00
Total	$431,677.03	$231,677.03	$200,000.00	

People who buy a home and then move a few years later are often surprised to find that their mortgage payments have barely dented the amount they still owe. They have not been cheated. Each month, they paid the interest due on their loan, fairly calculated, and every dollar beyond that did reduce their loan. What they don't realize is that an amortized loan does not reduce the unpaid balance equally each month because more interest is due in the beginning when the loan is large, and less is due at the end when the loan is small.

Comparing Loans: The Total-Payments Error

Truth in Lending laws require lenders to tell borrowers the total amount (principal plus interest) that they will pay over the life of the loan. Unfortunately, the prominent display of this information encourages borrowers to make the mistake of judging loans by the total payments. If the total payments are $240,000 for one loan and $320,000 for another, then the second loan must be much more expensive. Money is money, right? How could this be a mistake? Because it doesn't take into account *when* the payments are made. If you have to repay a dollar, would you rather pay it today or 10 years from now? Obviously 10 years from now because that allows you to earn interest for 10 years before you have to part with your dollar. Time is money.

It is not only unwary borrowers who fall into the total payments trap; so do some otherwise sensible advisers. *Consumer Reports* compared two alternatives for purchasing a washing machine, dryer, and automatic dishwasher for a new home:

1.   Buy from a store for $675, financed by a 2-year loan at a 15% interest rate.
2.   Buy from the home builder for $450, financed by a 27-year loan at a 7.75% interest rate.

The total payments are $1,075 with the builder or $785 with the store. *Consumer Reports* concluded that "the appliances would cost $290 more from the builder than from the store."

If the builder charges a third less for the appliances and half the interest rate, how can the store's offer be the better deal? It isn't. *Consumer Reports* erred by comparing the total payments, ignoring the fact that the payments to the store must be made during the next 2 years, while the payments to the builder are spread over 27 years. In the eyes of *Consumer Reports*, time isn't money; a dollar paid today is the same as a dollar paid 27 years from now.

If you just compare total payments, borrowing for 1 year at a 29 percent interest rate is better than borrowing for 30 years at a 1 percent interest rate. What do you think? The answer is obvious, but not to *Consumer Reports*!

The Right Way to Think About Loans

A simple comparison of total payments says that you are always better off borrowing less money and repaying the loan as soon as possible, because this reduces your total payments. In fact, a consumer finance book advised borrowers to reduce their costs by doing just that: Make the largest down payment you can afford and repay the loan as soon as possible. The very best strategy, according to a total-payments analysis, is to never borrow any money at all—no matter what the loan rate!

If you take into account the time value of money, then you reach a very different conclusion. Remember our earlier discussion: It is profitable to borrow at 6 percent in order to invest at 10 percent, and it is unprofitable to borrow at 6 percent in order to invest at 2 percent. This reasoning implies that if the loan rate is favorable, you want to borrow as much as you can for as long as you can.

Now, armed with this principle, you can answer the questions at the beginning of this chapter about borrowing.

1. If you can pay cash, does it make sense to take out a car loan? Yes, if the interest rate on the car loan is less than the rate of return you will earn on your cash. Otherwise, no.
2. If you can afford to make a $50,000 down payment on a house, does it make sense to make a $30,000 down payment and keep $20,000 invested in stocks? Yes, if the rate of return on your stocks is higher than the mortgage rate. Otherwise, no.
3. If you can afford to pay off part or all of your mortgage early, should you do so? Keep your mortgage if the rate of return on your investments is higher than your mortgage rate. Otherwise, prepay.

Let's spend a little more time on that third question because it crops up so frequently. Chapter 1, "The Million-Dollar Question," explained that paying off a 6 percent mortgage is like making an investment that pays 6 percent interest. Therefore, if you have a 6 percent mortgage and money in the bank earning only 4 percent, taking money out of the bank and paying down your mortgage is profitable.

Two other factors should be considered as well. First, you might want to leave some money in the bank if there is a chance you will need it for something else. Second, if you have trouble saving, an automatic plan for paying down your mortgage is one way to force yourself to save.

Bad News, You Won the Lottery

A realtor once made this odd argument. Mike won a $150,000 house in a lottery, but he doesn't have the $75,000 cash that he needs to pay the taxes on his winnings. If Mike takes out a mortgage in order to pay his taxes, his total payments over 30 years will be more than $150,000. Therefore, Mike is better off without the prize!

The realtor's mistake is to compare the total mortgage payments over 30 years with the current value of the house. We know that we shouldn't simply add up the total dollars paid. That's the total-payments error. A dollar paid 30 years from now is not worth the same as a dollar today.

Mike certainly shouldn't walk away from the prize because he can always sell the house, pay the tax, and keep the difference. What is amazing is how often total-payments calculations lead to nonsensical decisions.

Should You Borrow at 12% to Invest at 7%?

An elderly couple recently bought a car and asked the dealer if they could pay cash. After the dealer said, "Of course," they opened a bag they were carrying and poured dollar bills onto his desk. That will work.

You can also pay cash for a car by writing a check or using a credit card. Buyers who try to pay cash are sometimes dissuaded by sales managers who claim that the buyer can save hundreds of dollars by leaving their cash in the bank and borrowing from the car dealer. For example, when Mary Hernandez said she was going to pay $12,000 cash for a car, the sales manager told her she would be better off leaving her $12,000 in the bank earning 7 percent and borrowing from the car dealer at 12 percent.

Here is his persuasive, but fallacious, argument. If the $12,000 is kept in the bank for 4 years, the total interest, compounded monthly, comes to $3,864. The total interest on the amortized car loan is only $3,168. How can 7 percent interest be more than 12 percent interest? Can you figure out the scam?

The gimmick is that the loan is amortized, so that $12,000 is only borrowed for the first month. After that, each monthly payment covers the interest due and also reduces the unpaid balance until it hits zero at the end of the last month. Instead of borrowing $12,000 for 4 years, the car buyer borrows $12,000 at the beginning and almost nothing at the end, so the average amount borrowed over 4 years is about half the initial loan. This is the sales manager's trick: comparing 7 percent interest on $12,000 with 12 percent interest on roughly half of $12,000.

But this apples-and-oranges comparison is illogical. If Mary follows the sales manager's advice, she won't earn interest on the entire $12,000 for 4 years since she must take money out of the bank every month to make her car payments.

Month after month, the bank-account balance declines as Mary pays off her car loan. Her bank balance hits zero well before the car loan is paid off. Intuition is right. She must lose money paying 12 percent on the car loan and earning 7 percent on the bank account.

Mary couldn't pinpoint the flaw in the sales manager's numbers, but her intuition guided her to the right decision. She paid cash for the car.

The Bottom Line

1. Loans create leverage, multiplying gains and losses.
2. You will make money borrowing at 6 percent to invest at 10 percent; you will lose money borrowing at 6 percent to invest at 2 percent.
3. Amortized loan payments pay the interest on the outstanding balance and also pay down the balance until the loan is fully repaid.
4. Judging a loan by the total payments is a mistake because it doesn't take into account the timing. A dollar paid today is more expensive than a dollar paid 20 years from now.

6

Choosing the Right Mortgage

When you get a mortgage to buy a home, you must make choices about the size of your down payment, whether to have a 15-year or 30-year mortgage, whether to have a fixed rate or adjustable rate loan, and whether to choose a loan with points. This chapter explains the different loan options and helps you choose the best mortgage for your needs.

Finding a Lender

Traditionally, home buyers applied for mortgages at a local bank or savings and loan association (S&L), often the same bank where they had checking and savings accounts. Indeed, that's what banks do. They use money deposited in checking and savings accounts to make loans. Banks borrow money from their depositors to lend money to home buyers and other borrowers.

When you apply for a mortgage, the bank looks at your income to see if you can afford the monthly mortgage payments. A red flag is raised if the mortgage payments, homeowner's insurance, and property taxes are more than 40 percent of your before-tax income. Red flags could also fly if you have lots of other debts, have a spotty employment history, or have fallen behind or defaulted on other loans.

The bank also checks out the home to see if it is good collateral for the loan. An independent appraiser will walk through the home, measure the square footage, and use comps to estimate the market value of the property. Red flags fly if the appraiser's estimate is substantially below the price you have agreed to pay for the home.

If no red flags are flying, the bank will likely approve the loan and supply the money at the closing, which is when the seller gets paid and you get title to the home and a mortgage to pay for it. You then make monthly mortgage payments to the bank.

Nowadays, the process is pretty much the same, except that borrowers are not restricted to local banks. Using the telephone and the Internet, you can borrow from lenders anywhere in the country, indeed anywhere in the world. Many nationwide lenders (like Citibank and Chase) post their rates on the Internet. Some, like ING Direct, don't have local branches where people can deposit money or apply for loans; everything is done online, over the phone, or by mail.

You can also deal with a mortgage broker who will contact several lenders on your behalf. The broker gets a piece of the action for this service, which naturally comes out of your pocket. The benefit is that the broker does a lot of the work for you and might be able to find a better deal than you could find on your own.

Another change is that banks and other lenders don't necessarily hold on to your mortgage for the duration of the loan. Instead, they often sell their mortgages to Fannie Mae, Freddie Mac, and other institutional investors who either hold them in their portfolios or bundle them with other loans into mortgage-backed securities that are sold to mutual funds, Wall Street firms, and other investors. If this happens to your loan, you will get a letter in the mail saying that your loan has been sold and instructing you where to send your mortgage payments.

Getting Pre-Approved

Most people don't apply for a mortgage until after they find a home they like and their offer is accepted. But you can actually apply for a loan before you find a home to buy. This is called pre-approval because your loan is approved prior to the purchase. You are not obligated to borrow any or all of the money, or even to borrow from this lender. If you are pre-approved for $300,000, you might find that you only need to borrow $260,000, or you might decide to wait until better homes come on the market, or you might find a lender with a better interest rate.

One advantage of a pre-approved loan is that you know the maximum amount that you can afford to pay for a home: your down payment plus the pre-approved loan. Having a pre-approved loan also makes your offer more credible. Put yourself in the seller's shoes. If you were selling your house and had two comparable offers, one with a pre-approved loan and the other contingent on the buyer being approved for a mortgage, which would you choose? The one with the pre-approved loan, of course. So, when you are on the buyer's side of the table, you want to be the one with the pre-approved loan. Pre-approval also convinces real estate agents that you are a serious buyer.

Here is what you do to get pre-approved. First, call some lenders or mortgage brokers and shop around until you find the best interest rate. Once you choose a lender, they will ask you to fill out a loan application that describes your employment history (so they can see if you have a stable job); your income (so they can see if you can afford the monthly mortgage payments); and your assets (so they can see where the down payment is coming from). They will also ask you to authorize a credit check so they can see if you have a history of paying your bills on time.

Second, gather the paperwork to document your loan application: your recent pay stubs, tax returns, and bank statements. If all is in order, you should have your answer in a few weeks. Your pre-approval letter will say that you have been approved for a mortgage of a certain amount, say $300,000. Your pre-approval usually has a time limit on it and is subject to you finding a home with an acceptable appraisal and clear title, so there will be no dispute over who should be paid for the property.

Make sure that your pre-approval letter states that you are officially approved for a loan of a specified amount. Some letters look like pre-approval letters, but aren't. A conditional pre-approval letter, or pre-qualified letter, simply estimates how much you might be able to borrow based on your application form. A pre-qualified letter states that the loan is conditional on the lender verifying your financial situation. The lender hasn't made a commitment to lend you anything and may well decide not to approve your loan. A conditional approval is obviously not as convincing as an actual loan approval—to yourself, to realtors, and to home sellers.

Here's another warning: You can call several places to ask about loans and to find out what terms lenders are offering, but don't go all the way through the application process with multiple lenders. If several lenders run credit checks on you, this can reduce your credit score because each credit check suggests you are thinking of borrowing more money.

And a final warning: Be sure to use Tables 5.1 and 5.2 to do your own calculations to confirm that you really can afford the loan that has been approved. Some aggressive lenders will loan you more than you can realistically afford to borrow. Why? Because they are paid commissions based on the volume of loans they "sell." The more loans they approve, the more they get paid. The company they work for may sell the loan to someone else and, if you cannot make your payments, it is no longer their problem.

It is your problem, though. It is better for you to be too cautious than to be too aggressive because it will be an emotional and financial disaster if you are unable to make your mortgage payments.

Saving for Your Down Payment

If you buy a $200,000 home with a $160,000 mortgage, the remaining $40,000 is your down payment, which you pay at the closing when you receive the title to the home. The down payment protects the lender, because your home is collateral for your mortgage. In this example, as long as the bank can sell your home for at least $160,000, it can get back the money it loaned you. Obviously, the bigger the down payment, the more protection there is for the bank.

For many people, the biggest obstacle to buying a home is the initial down payment; $40,000 is a lot of money! Once you get past this hurdle and buy your first home, the profits you make on your home usually provide the down payment on your next home. This is why your first home is often called a starter home. You start with a small home, invest your home dividends and build up equity, and then trade up until you have your dream home. As the saying goes, "The rich get richer, but how do you get rich in the first place?" Answer: by putting together enough money for a down payment.

You might need less money for a down payment than you think. The traditional rule was that a down payment should equal 20 percent of the purchase price: $20,000 on a $100,000 home; $40,000 on a $200,000 home; and $80,000 on a $400,000 home. Some lenders may require only a 10 percent or 5 percent down payment, particularly if the loan qualifies for Federal Housing Administration (FHA) insurance. Another great option is Veterans Affairs (VA) insurance, which requires no money down. In each case, you apply for a loan from a bank or other lender and the lender gets federal insurance if you meet the eligibility requirements.

Less well known are special loan programs from state housing agencies. These are typically nonprofit organizations that were originally set up with government assistance, but now operate largely independent of the state government. These agencies raise money by issuing tax-exempt bonds. Because the bonds are tax-exempt, these agencies can raise money cheaply and can charge lower interest rates on their mortgages. To qualify for this tax-exempt status, these agencies are generally designed to help those who need help; for example, first-time buyers, buyers with low-to-moderate income, or people buying homes in designated target areas. These programs vary greatly from state to state, so check with your state government.

Another way to get money for a down payment is to borrow money from your parents or grandparents. If your parents bought a home many years ago, they might have built up considerable equity in their home and they may have used their home dividends to build up a large investment portfolio. If so, they might be willing to use a home equity loan or take money out of their investment portfolio to lend you the money you need for your down payment.

Your parents might have bought their first home the same way, by borrowing money from their parents; now they are doing for you what their parents did for them. Many years from now, you can do the same for your children.

You should view your parents' help as a loan, not a gift. If they took money out of a money market fund, pay them the same interest rate they were earning on this fund. If they used a home equity loan, pay them the same interest rate they are paying on their home equity loan. It is easier for everyone if your parents can view their help as an investment. After you have bought your house, use your home dividend to pay off your parents' loan as soon as possible. You don't want to start a family war because your parents considered it a loan, but you never gave them back their money.

One exception to this rule is when your parents got their down payment as a gift from their parents. They are likely to feel that this is a family tradition that they should continue (and that you should continue with your children).

Another way to get enough money for a down payment is to save some money each month and let compound interest carry you to your down-payment goal. If you don't seem to have much money left at the end of each month, do your saving at the beginning of each month. As soon as you get your paycheck, put $100 or more in a money market fund or brokerage account. Call this your down-payment fund so that you are absolutely clear that this fund is not to be raided for impulsive purchases. Don't touch your down-payment fund until you use it as a down payment.

To make this work, you must say no to credit-card debt. If you currently have some debt, use your monthly savings to pay this off as quickly as possible. Then keep your credit-card debt at zero and use your monthly savings to build up your down-payment fund. Don't use your credit card to "make up" for the money going into your down-payment fund. This will just dig a deeper and deeper hole, because the interest rate you pay on credit-card debt is higher than the interest rate you earn on your down-payment fund. Saving $100 means saving $100, not borrowing $100.

Table 6.1 shows how quickly a disciplined monthly savings plan can build up your down-payment fund. Saving $300 a month for five years will give you $20,427, which is enough for a 20 percent down payment on a $100,000 home or a 10 percent down payment on a $200,000 home. The calculations in Table 6.1 assume a conservative 5 percent return on your money. If you invest some of your money in a stock index fund that earns a higher return, your down-payment fund will grow even faster.

The more you save, the faster you will get to your down-payment goal. But even $100 a month will work. What is $100 a month? About $3 a day. Surely you can save $3 a day by cutting back on a few indulgences. Fewer visits to Starbucks. Fewer pizza deliveries. Fewer trips to movie theaters. Fewer restaurant meals or a few less drinks and desserts when you go out. Think of it this way: you are going to give up a few indulgences for a few years, and in return you will get a home to call your own and potentially increase your wealth by hundreds of thousands of dollars—which will buy a lot more indulgences than you are sacrificing now.

Table 6.1 Saving for A Down Payment, with a 5% Return

	$100/month	$300/month	$500/month
5 years	$6,809	$20,427	$34,045
10 years	$15,499	$46,498	$77,496

You can also make big-bucks additions to your down-payment fund. The next time you buy a car, you can save thousands of dollars by buying a sensible car instead of a show-off car. Show off later, when you own your dream home and are saving thousands of dollars by not paying rent. Buy the sensible car and put the money you save by not buying the show-off car in your down-payment fund.

Instead of spending thousands of dollars on vacations this year, put thousands of dollars in your down-payment fund. If you get an annual bonus, put it in your down-payment fund. If you inherit money, put it in your down-payment fund. The more money you put in and the sooner you do it, the sooner you will be ready to buy a home.

We are not thrilled about the idea of taking money out of your IRA to make a down payment. But sometimes it makes sense, especially if you don't have any good alternatives. Chapter 10, "Letting Your Home Take Care of You," explains why your home can be a Home Retirement Account (HRA) that is as profitable as an IRA. The government evidently feels the same way. If you are a first-time home buyer, you can withdraw up to $10,000 from your IRA for a down payment without incurring a 10 percent penalty for early withdrawal. (But you still have to pay income taxes on the money you withdraw.)

Nonetheless, we hesitate to recommend this option because if you have trouble saving, raiding an IRA is an unhelpful precedent. You should own a home and you should also own stocks, bonds, and other financial assets.

Mortgage Terms

Table 6.2 compares the average terms for fixed-rate mortgages on new homes in 1970, 1980, 1990, 2000, and 2010. The average home price increased at an annual rate of about 6 percent over this period. Mortgage rates have gone up and down with other interest rates. Interestingly, even though home prices have increased greatly, the drop in mortgage rates since 1980 reduced the ratio of the annual mortgage payments to median (middle) household income from 46.5 percent in 1980 to 32.5 percent in 2010.

Table 6.2 Average Mortgage Terms on New Homes

	1970	1980	1990	2000	2010
Price	$35,500	$83,500	$153,200	$234,500	$333,900
Mortgage	$25,200	$59,300	$112,400	$177,000	$240,700
Years	25.1	28.2	27.3	29.2	28.4
Interest rate	8.27%	12.25%	9.68%	7.41	4.70
Monthly payment	$199	$626	$977	$1,236	$1,278
Median Income	$7,466	$16,166	$27,792	$40,199	$47,222
payment income	32.0%	46.5%	42.2%	36.9%	32.5%

Mortgage Rates

When a bank lends you money to buy a house, they are investing in your mortgage, the same way the bank might invest in U. S. Treasury bonds. Figure 6.1 shows the average annual interest rates on mortgages and Treasury bonds from 1960 through 2012.

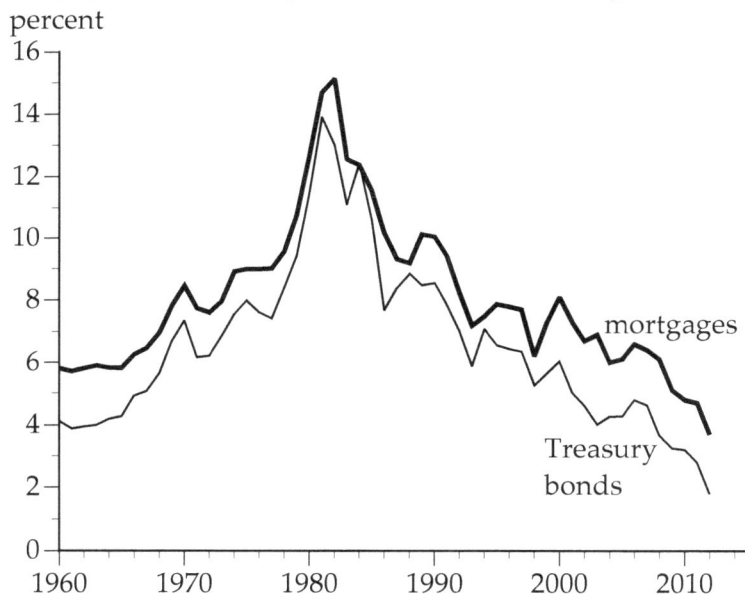

Figure 6.1 Mortgage rates and Treasury bond interest rates

Mortgage rates are higher than Treasury bond rates because mortgages are not as safe as Treasury bonds. Nonetheless, mortgage rates and bond rates generally move up and down together because investors think mortgages and bonds are competing investments. If mortgage rates were a lot higher than Treasury rates, investors would switch to mortgages. If mortgage rates were lower than Treasury rates, investors would switch to Treasury bonds. Mortgage rates consequently rise and fall with Treasury rates and other interest rates.

Anchoring

Anchoring is a general human tendency to rely on a reference point when making decisions. For example, people tend to judge whether they are getting a good deal on a car by comparing the final negotiated price to the dealer's initial price, no matter how unrealistic the price. Thus, good salesmen starts with a high price.

Anchoring shows up in a variety of guises in real estate. Some people use the price they paid for their house as an anchor for its current value: "This house can't really be worth $400,000 because we bought it for $200,000." People also use comps as anchors. "The house across the street sold for $400,000 two years ago; we're not selling our house for less than $400,000." This anchoring is one reason why home prices usually don't drop much when the housing market slows; instead, sellers wait until the market recovers.

People also use anchoring to gauge whether interest rates are high or low. Greg and Jane Landon bought their first house in Eugene, Oregon, in 1971. Figure 6.2 shows that going back to at least 1920, mortgage rates had never been above 6 percent until they broke the 6 percent barrier in 1966 and hit 7.5 percent in 1971.

Greg thought they should wait until mortgage rates went back down to "normal" levels; that is, below 6 percent. Greg was using past mortgage rates as an anchor to gauge what mortgage rates "should be."

But interest rates aren't governed by physical laws, like gravity or magnetism, that force them to behave in easily predictable ways. Just because mortgage rates had been 6 percent in the past doesn't mean they will be 6 percent again anytime soon. Jane persuaded Greg that they should stop renting and buy a home to call their own. Greg grimaced and they borrowed at 7.5 percent to buy a starter home.

Seven years later, in 1978, they moved to Houston, Texas, and mortgage rates were now 9.6 percent (see Figure 6.3).

Greg was now even more certain that they should wait for mortgage rates to return to "normal." But the value of their Oregon home had doubled and, at that time, sellers had to pay a 35 percent capital gains tax on the profit they made from their homes, unless the seller purchased a new home—in which case the capital gain was rolled over and the tax was deferred, perhaps indefinitely. So Greg gritted his teeth and they bought a home in Houston with a 9.6 percent mortgage.

Mortgage rate, percent

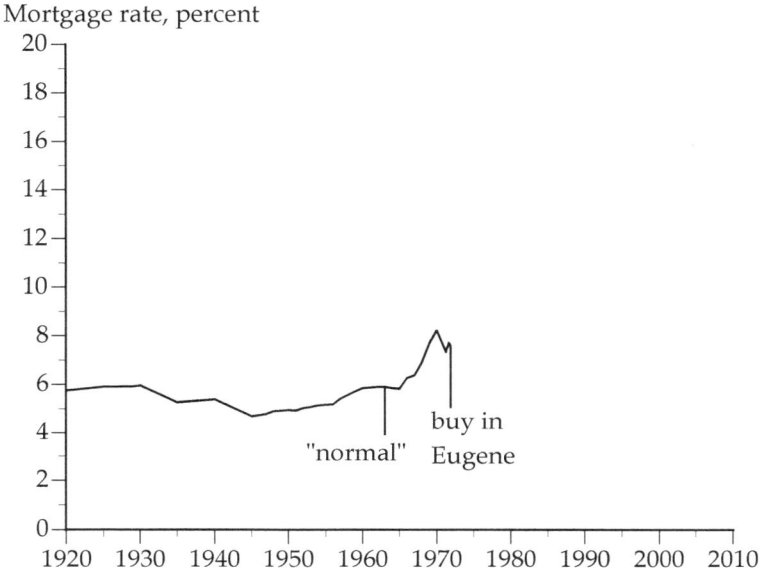

Figure 6.2 The Landons buy their first home,
when mortgage rates are high

Mortgage rate, percent

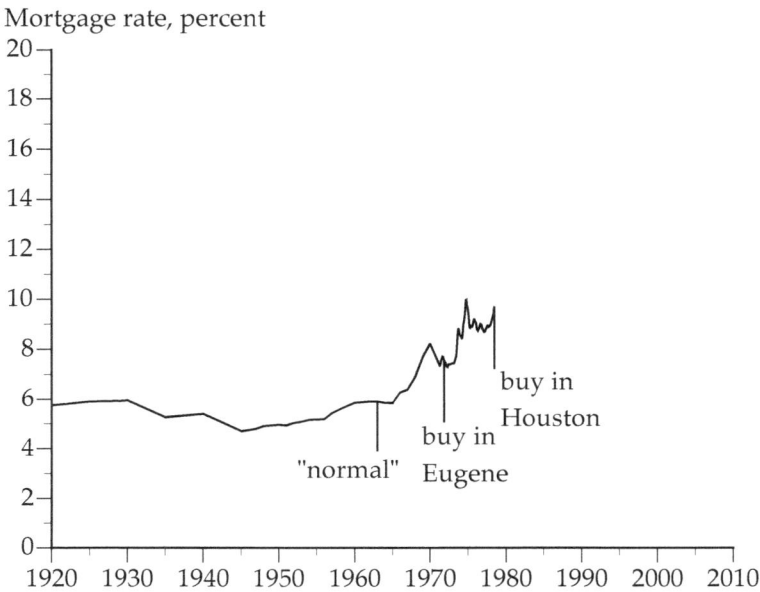

Figure 6.3 The Landons buy their second home,
when mortgages rates are even higher

Three years later, in 1981, they moved to Seattle, Washington. Now they would have to pay a capital gains tax on the gain on their Eugene house plus the gain on their Houston house unless they bought another house. They didn't want to pay this capital gains tax, but now mortgage rates were above 17 percent (Figure 6.4).

Fortunately, Greg's new company had a mortgage plan that would lend employees money at an 8.7 percent interest rate. Greg was much happier with 8.7 percent than with 17 percent, but he still thought they would be better off if they waited for mortgage rates to return to normal. The deciding factor was the annoying capital gains tax they would have to pay if they didn't buy a home. So, they bought a home in Seattle with an 8.7 percent mortgage.

Mortgage rate, percent

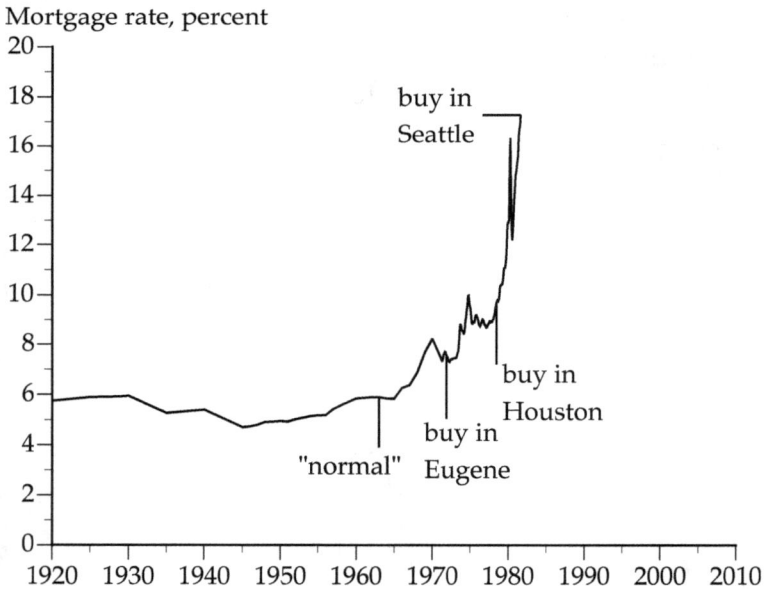

Figure 6.4 The Landons buy their third home,
when mortgages rates are even higher

Finally, in 2003 mortgage rates fell below 6 percent (Figure 6.5). Mortgage rates had returned to normal, just like Greg had predicted! But it took 40 years to do so. If the Landons had waited to buy a home until mortgage rates fell below 6 percent, they would have missed out on the best investments they ever made: their homes in Eugene, Houston, and Seattle.

Mortgage rate, percent

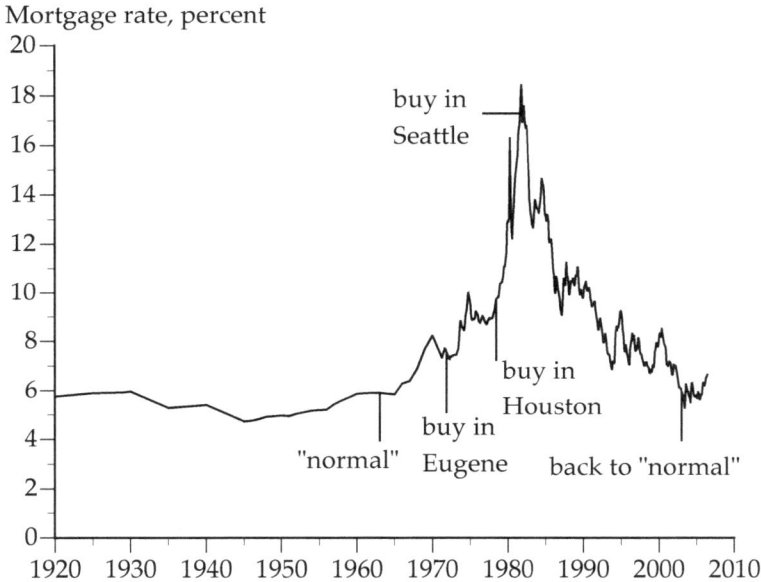

Figure 6.5 Mortgage rates finally return to normal

The moral of this story is: Don't try to time the real estate market. Predicting home prices and interest rates is very difficult. Instead, use the principles explained in Chapters 2, "Your Home is an Investment" and 3 "Now is a Good Time to Own a Home" to determine if buying a home now makes sense. Is this home really worth the price? If it is, buy it.

Mortgage Points

During the 1960s and most of the 1970s, mortgage rates averaged about 2 percentage points above the interest rates on U. S. Treasury bonds. However, when Treasury rates rose to double digits in the early 1980s, many banks bumped up against state usury laws that capped mortgage rates at 10 percent. Some banks stopped making mortgage loans and bought bonds instead. Others discovered that they could get around usury ceilings by charging points, a fee equal to a specified percentage of the loan. For example, if you borrow $100,000 at 6 percent plus 5 points, you only receive $95,000 ($100,000 minus the 5 percent points), but pay 6 percent interest on the full $100,000 loan.

Because you pay interest on $100,000, but only get $95,000, the effective interest rate is obviously somewhat higher than 6 percent. On a 30-year mortgage, 5 points raises the effective interest rate by about half a percentage point, from 6 percent to 6.49 percent.

What if you change jobs, marry, divorce, have children, or for some other reason decide to pay off the mortgage before 30 years pass? Table 6.3 shows that repaying a mortgage early shortens the loan and increases the effective interest rate.

Table 6.3 Effective Interest Rate on a 30-Year Mortgage
with a 6 percent Interest Rate and 5 Points

Year Repaid	Effective Interest Rate (Percent)
1	11.34
2	8.77
3	7.90
4	7.48
5	7.23
10	6.74
20	6.52
30	6.49

Clearly, points can be very expensive, especially if you repay your loans after only a few years. You are usually better off with a mortgage that has a slightly higher interest rate and no points.

In Chapter 7, "Refinancing and Home Equity Loans," we discuss prepayment penalties, which are like points except they are added on when you prepay your mortgage. Like points, they raise the effective interest rate on your loan. Like points, avoid them if you can.

Sure, I'll Lend You Money

Several years ago, a study of mortgage lending in Bridgeport, Connecticut, discovered an astonishing loan. It was a $17,000 30-year conventional amortized loan. So far, so good. The interest rate was 18 percent, plus $6,460 in points. The borrower was paying 18 percent interest on a $17,000 loan but only received $10,540.

The effective loan rate was 29 percent. The borrower was evidently desperate or ill-informed. The lender should have been ashamed (or prosecuted).

30-Years, 15-Years, or ?

In September 2007, average mortgage rates in the United States were 5.8 percent on a 15-year mortgage and 6.1 percent on a 30-year mortgage. How would you choose between them? There is no way to know for certain which option will turn out to be more profitable, but you can make a reasonable choice.

First, the monthly payments will be higher on a short-term loan because you are paying it off quicker. For example, on a $200,000 loan, the monthly payments are $1,222 for a 30-year loan at 6.1 percent and $1,666 for a 15-year loan at 5.8 percent. Offsetting these higher payments, of course, is that you are done with the shorter loan after 15 years. Second, if you can afford the higher monthly payments, you are usually better off borrowing at a low interest rate. Ten-year and fifteen-year mortgages usually have lower rates than thirty-year mortgages, which is a good reason for choosing a shorter-term mortgage.

A surprising number of people instinctively prefer 30-year mortgages even though the interest rates are higher. Maybe this is because these were the standard mortgages for so many years. Or maybe this is because it sounds so reassuring to have the mortgage rate fixed for such a long period of time. But why pay a high interest rate to get a mortgage that will last longer than you plan to stay in your home?

Claire was 30 years old and single when she purchased a 2-bedroom, 1-bath home, with one of the bedrooms used as a home office. She planned to marry and start a family in 5 to 10 years, ideally with two children. This home didn't fit her long-term plans and, yet, her first instinct was to choose a 30-year mortgage because that's what her parents had. Buying a starter home was a good idea. She didn't need anything bigger at the time and building up equity in a home is better than paying rent. However, 10-year mortgage rates were significantly lower than 30-year mortgage rates and she could easily afford the higher monthly payments with a 10-year mortgage. If she will move to a different home in ten years, then she has no compelling reason to get anything longer than a 10-year mortgage. She chose the 10-year mortgage.

Emily lived in rent-controlled housing in the northeast all her life. At age 75, she decided to move to Arizona to be closer to her children and grandchildren. Emily bought a nice 1-bedroom condominium and initially insisted on a 30-year mortgage because she "liked the safety" of having the mortgage rate fixed for 30 years. We admire her optimism, but the odds were against her living to 105. At the time, a 15-year mortgage would reduce her mortgage rate by half a percentage point. Her pension and Social Security income could easily cover the monthly payments. She chose the 15-year mortgage.

Adjustable Rate Loans

So far, we have been talking about fixed rate mortgages, where the interest rate is set for the life of the loan—perhaps 30 years. With an adjustable rate mortgage (ARM), in contrast, the interest rate on the mortgage goes up and down with other interest rates. The widespread use of adjustable rate mortgages was first permitted in April 1981, and during the next 5 years roughly half of all new mortgages were adjustable-rate.

These flexible rate loans go by a variety of names: adjustable rate, variable rate, and so on. In each case, the lender periodically adjusts the loan rate to reflect current interest rates. Here are some of the key features to consider.

1. The rate is typically adjusted every year after a specified number of years. For example, on a 3/1 ARM, the rate is fixed for three years and is adjusted every year after that. The longer the fixed period, the better.
2. The adjustable interest rate is equal to a specified base rate, such as the 1-year Treasury rate plus a margin (typically 2% to 3%). For example, suppose the adjustable rate is equal to the 1-year Treasury rate plus a 2.5 percent margin. If the Treasury rate is 4.2 percent, the adjustable rate is 4.2 + 2.5 = 6.7 percent. The smaller the margin the better.
3. Most ARMs have caps that limit the rate adjustment to, say, 2 percent in any given year and 5 percent during the life of the mortgage. The tighter the caps, the better.

In general, is it more financially advantageous to have a fixed rate mortgage or an adjustable rate mortgage? Ignoring risk for the moment, the crucial question is whether the average value of the adjustable interest rate will be higher or lower than the fixed interest rate. Suppose the fixed rate is 6 percent and a 5/1 ARM has a 5.5 percent rate for the first five years, after which it is adjusted annually. A useful rule of thumb is that the ARM will be cheaper if the average value of the adjustable rate is less than 6 percent.

Of course, interest rates are hard to forecast and risk might be an important concern. You don't want to lose your home because your mortgage payments go up more than you can afford to pay. On the other hand, the likelihood that your income will increase as time passes partly offsets the risk that your mortgage payments might increase significantly. If your income increases by 5 percent a year, it will be 28 percent higher after five years, and 63 percent higher after ten years. This cushion may well absorb rising mortgage payments.

Suppose, for example, that you have a $5,000 monthly income and take out a $200,000 5/1 ARM at an initial 6 percent interest rate. The $1,199 monthly payments are 24 percent of your monthly income:

$$\frac{\$1,199}{\$5,000} = 0.24$$

If the interest rate goes up to 7 percent after five years, the monthly payments will increase to $1,349, but your monthly income is now $6,381, and the ratio of monthly payments to income falls to 21.1 percent:

$$\frac{\$1,349}{\$6,381} = 0.21$$

If you have a comfortable cushion (and you should!), you may be able to afford modest increases in the adjustable rate and enjoy decreases in the adjustable rate. If you can afford fluctuating mortgage payments, then you are back to the question of whether the average value for the adjustable rate will be higher or lower than the fixed rate.

Another consideration is whether you might move after a few years, which makes the security of a fixed rate mortgage irrelevant. If, for example, you have a 5/1 ARM and you move after 5 years, your adjustable rate mortgage is effectively a fixed rate mortgage—which makes it easy to choose between a 5.5 percent 5/1 ARM and a 6 percent 30-year mortgage.

Watch out for adjustable rate loans with artificially low teaser rates that make a mortgage seem more affordable than it really is. For example, the interest rate might be 4 percent for the first year or two and then rise to the one-year Treasury rate plus 6 percent. The initial 4 percent rate makes the loan affordable for people who realistically cannot afford to make the monthly payments when the rate adjusts to 10, 11, or 12 percent. The only way out of this predicament is if their incomes increase drastically or if home prices rise fast enough for them to sell their home for a quick profit before the mortgage rate adjusts. Sometimes everything works out and people are able to buy homes that they couldn't otherwise afford. Too often, though, people can't make their payments and lose their homes. So-called subprime borrowers who lose their homes deserve better. Don't be one of them.

Creative Financing

In the 1970s and early 1980s, the lethal combination of inflation and the Federal Reserve's efforts to wring inflation out of the economy drove interest rates skyward. Meanwhile, the federal government did not allow banks to pay their depositors competitive interest rates. Banks gave away dishes, toasters, and even color television sets. But they still lost depositors.

These credit crunches battered the housing market. Banks raised mortgage rates to unprecedented levels and, even then, rejected loan applications because they had no money to lend. Home buyers were discouraged by high mortgage rates and rejected loan applications. Home sellers were discouraged by the lack of buyers.

In this environment, buyers and sellers turned to creative financing, novel ways of borrowing money to buy homes. Creative financing typically involves owner financing, with the buyer borrowing money from the seller at, say, 12 percent rather than from a bank at 18 percent. The buyer appreciates the lower interest rate and the seller is relieved to have sold the house. In 1980 and 1981, roughly half of all sales of existing homes involved some sort of creative financing.

Buying a House with Creative Financing

Here is a fairly typical real estate transaction that was made in 1980 in Amherst, New Hampshire. At the time, Amherst banks were charging a minimum of 18 percent on new mortgages and rejecting most mortgage applications. Gregg Andrews was eager to move and offered to sell his home for $66,000 to Lucille Burns, with Lucille putting $30,000 down and borrowing $36,000 from Gregg at 10 percent for 10 years.

What is the value of this below-market loan to Lucille? The 10 percent rate is substantially below the 18 percent charged by banks; but it is only a 10-year loan. Is this deal worth hundreds or thousands of dollars? This owner financing was equivalent to a $10,000 price cut in that Lucille would be able to make these same payments if Gregg reduced the price by $10,000 and Lucille borrowed from a bank at an 18 percent interest rate. Stated somewhat differently, the 10 percent interest rate allowed Lucille to borrow $10,000 more than she could have borrowed with an 18 percent interest rate, with the same monthly payments. Lucille accepted Gregg's creative financing offer and bought this house.

You can evaluate a creative financing deal in the same way, by comparing how much you can borrow with the owner's financing to how much you can borrow with traditional bank financing. Table 6.4 shows some calculations for a 30-year amortized loan. For example, if you can borrow from a bank at 8 percent, you can borrow 22.4 percent more money and have the same monthly payments if the owner agrees to lend you money at 6 percent. The savings are somewhat smaller if you repay your loan early, but owner financing can still be a great deal—for the buyer.

Table 6.4 Additional Amount (Percent) That Can
be Borrowed with Owner Financing

Owner Interest Rate (Percent)	Bank Interest Rate (Percent)			
	5	6	7	8
7				10.3%
6			11.0%	22.4%
5		11.7%	23.9%	36.7%
4	12.4%	25.6%	39.4%	53.7%

Biweekly Mortgages

In a *biweekly mortgage*, monthly payments are calculated as if it were a conventional 30-year amortized monthly mortgage, but half this monthly amount is paid every other week. For example, with a $100,000 30-year mortgage at a 9.25 percent interest rate, the monthly payments are $822. With a biweekly, the borrower pays $411 every other week and the loan is paid off in less than 22 years. The total payments are $296,165 with monthly payments and $231,996 with biweekly payments. Money for nothing! Some people sell this "secret," claiming that it is a trick bankers don't want you to know about. Fat chance. If lenders lost money on biweeklies, they wouldn't offer them.

Have you figured out the gimmick? Because there are 52 weeks in a year, you make 26 biweekly payments, each half the size of the 12 monthly payments. This amounts to one extra monthly payment a year. In addition, the $411 payment that is made after the first two weeks of the month reduces the loan balance on which interest is charged during the next 2 weeks. With less interest due, more of the payment goes to paying off the loan and the unpaid balance hits zero sooner. A biweekly has smaller total payments, but these payments are made sooner.

When discussing this exact example, a director of a large mortgage banking firm concluded that a 30-year loan with monthly payments would need a 6.7 percent interest rate to do as well as a biweekly paid over 22 years with a 9.25 percent mortgage rate. He was making the total payments error—adding up payments over 30 years and over 22 years, and assuming that it doesn't matter when the payments are made.

How would you choose between a 9.25 percent monthly and a 9.25 percent biweekly? The relevant question is whether you want to borrow money longer at a 9.25 percent interest rate. If you do, choose the 30-year monthly; if you don't, choose the biweekly. How would you choose between a 6.7 percent monthly and a 9.25 percent biweekly? Go with the lower interest rate, 6.7 percent.

Graduated Payment Loans

A conventional amortized loan has constant monthly payments for the life of the loan, typically 30 years. If your income rises over time, the monthly mortgage payment will be a much smaller fraction of your income at the end of the loan than at the beginning.

Imagine, for example, that you are just beginning your career at a $3,000 monthly salary and that your income will grow by 5 percent a year. If you borrow $200,000 at 6 percent, your mortgage payments will be $1,199, which is 40 percent of your income now but will be only 9 percent of your income 30 years from now. Doesn't it make more sense to have monthly mortgage payments that start low and then grow with your income?

As a practical matter, the mortgage payments might be such a large fraction of income in the early years that a young household cannot qualify for a mortgage even though it will have plenty of income later. One way to ease the financial burden on young households who expect their income to grow over time is with a graduated payment mortgage (GPM) in which the monthly payments are initially low and then grow along with income.

In our example, a graduated mortgage plan with mortgage payments growing by 5 percent a year would start with $673 a month and end with $2,772 a month, each 22 percent of household income. A graduated payment mortgage attempts to keep housing expenses at a relatively constant share of household income, making mortgages more accessible for people who expect their income to rise as time passes.

Figure 6.6 compares the monthly payments for a 30-year, $200,000 mortgage at a 6 percent annual interest rate when the monthly payments are constant and when they grow by 5 percent annually.

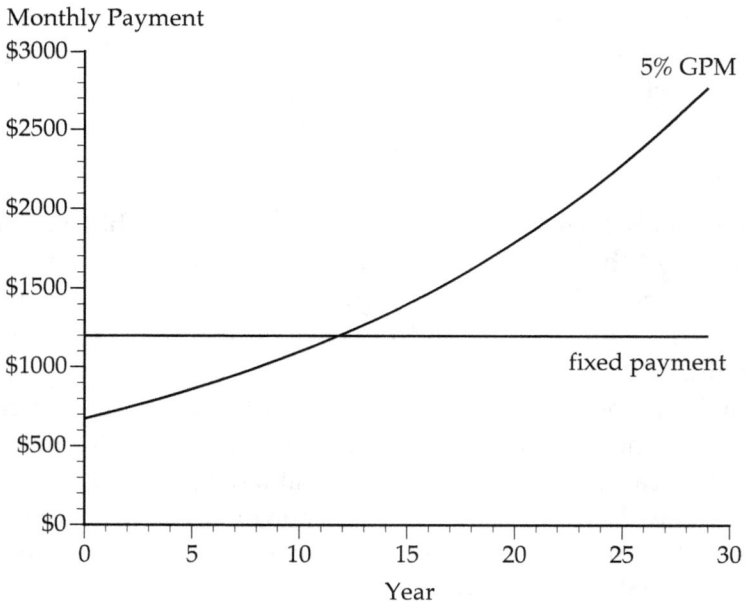

Figure 6.6 Monthly payments for a fixed payment mortgage and a 5 percent GPM.

Figure 6.7 shows these monthly payments as a fraction of income for a household whose monthly income is currently $3,000 and will increase by 5 percent annually. With constant monthly payments, the ratio of payments to income steadily declines; with the 5 percent graduated payment mortgage, the payments are a constant fraction of income.

In practice, if the early payments are not large enough to cover the interest due on the loan, negative amortization occurs for several years (the unpaid balance increases). A *BusinessWeek* article on GPMs treated negative amortization as a drawback and concluded that GPMs actually cost more than fixed payment mortgages in the long run. How do you suppose they reached that conclusion?

$$\frac{\text{Monthly payment}}{\text{Monthly income}}$$

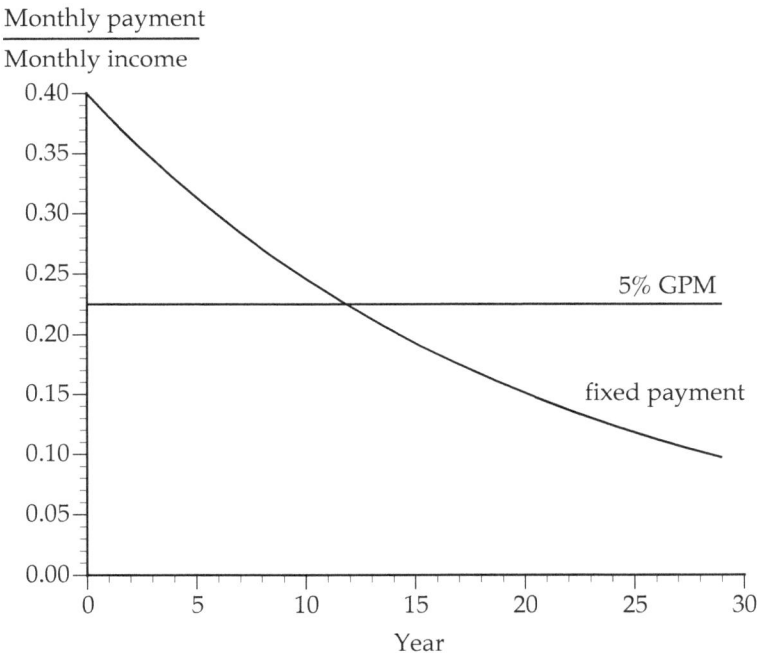

Figure 6.7 The ratio of monthly payments to monthly income

The total payments error again! The borrower pays more total interest with a GPM because the unpaid balance grows at first instead of declining, and you always pay more interest when you borrow more money. Here, your monthly payments are lower at the beginning and higher at the end, and *BusinessWeek* simply adds up the total payments, regardless of when they are made.   The correct way to think about a graduated payment mortgage is to ask whether you want to borrow more money to buy a home to live in and keep your monthly payments at a relatively constant fraction of your income. For some people, the answer is a resounding yes!

The people who have to be wary are those who can barely pay their bills even with lower initial payments and there is little realistic chance that their income will grow as fast as their mortgage payments. These are again subprime borrowers who do not qualify for conventional mortgages and, so, turn to alternatives that might work out, but often don't. Do not take a graduated payment mortgage unless you are certain that your future income will cover the higher payments ahead.

The Bottom Line

1. A down payment can be an intimidating hurdle. Do everything you can to clear this hurdle quickly.
2. Mortgage rates go up and down with other interest rates and are not easily predicted. Don't try to time mortgage rates by waiting for interest rates to fall.
3. Try to avoid loans with points, especially if you think you might move within 10 years.
4. Adjustable rate loans often have lower interest rates than fixed rate loans, but are risky if interest rates go up and you can't afford higher mortgage payments.
5. Creative financing involves a loan from the home seller at favorable terms, and is equivalent to a price cut.
6. Graduated payment loans can make loans affordable for people who are confident their income will grow substantially over time, but are a foreclosure waiting to happen if your income does not grow as fast as your mortgage payments.

7

Refinancing and Home Equity Loans

After you buy a home, you might rethink your mortgage for many reasons. If interest rates fall, should you refinance with a new mortgage at a lower interest rate? If you inherit some money, should you pay off your mortgage? If you remodel your kitchen, should you take out a home equity loan or refinance your mortgage? If you have used credit cards to buy things you couldn't resist, should you use a home equity loan to pay off your credit-card debt? Let's see.

Heads You Win, Tails I Lose

Although it's a bit of an exaggeration, people used to say that banking was as easy as 1, 2, 3: Pay your depositors 1 percent, charge your borrowers 2 percent, and be on the golf course by 3. In the 1960s and early 1970s, savings and loan associations (S&Ls) paid their depositors interest rates ranging from 2% to 5%, and loaned the money out in mortgages at 4% to 8%, which was enough to pay depositors, cover expenses, and make a profit, too. Mortgage rates hit an unprecedented 10 percent in 1978. Most observers thought that interest rates would soon fall to more normal levels. They were wrong. Interest rates went higher still, to over 18 percent in 1981, and people who borrowed at 10 percent were lucky to have what, in retrospect, were low-interest loans. The S&Ls they had borrowed from were not so lucky.

S&Ls had to raise deposit rates to double-digit levels to hold onto depositors, but were only earning single-digit interest on mortgages that were written in the 1960s and 1970s. The overall net worth of S&Ls fell from positive $23 billion at the end of 1977 to negative $44 billion at the end of 1981. The S&L industry went bankrupt because interest rates had risen unexpectedly!

And what if interest rates had fallen unexpectedly? S&Ls would have made enormous profits if they reduced deposit rates to 1 percent while collecting 8 percent interest on mortgages. But homeowners would not have kept those old high-interest mortgages. They would have refinanced by taking out new mortgages at the new low interest rates. S&Ls made a bad bet. Depositors could refinance if rates fell, but S&Ls could not renegotiate if rates rose. Heads, depositors win; tails, S&Ls lose.

When S&Ls realized how expensive this bad bet could be, they changed the rules of the game by revising their standard mortgage contracts in two important ways. First, they inserted due-on-sale clauses, which state that if the borrower sells the home, the mortgage must be repaid and cannot be passed on to the buyer. Second, to penalize borrowers who refinance when interest rates go down, S&Ls inserted prepayment penalties, additional charges that the borrower must pay the S&L if the loan is repaid early. Borrowers are not thrilled with prepayment penalties because most people don't stay in the same home for 30 years. In response to consumer complaints, many states have outlawed prepayment penalties. Some loans have soft penalties that don't apply if the loan is repaid after a waiting period of, say, 5 years or if the loan is repaid because the borrower sells the home.

Prepayment Penalties

To analyze the financial implications of prepayment penalties, let's analyze a 30-year, $100,000 mortgage at 6 percent with a 5 percent prepayment penalty. How does this penalty change the effective interest rate? The analysis is very similar to the case of mortgage points, the main difference being that points are tacked on at the beginning and prepayment penalties are added at the end. Table 7.1 shows the effective interest rate for different horizons.

If the loan is kept for 30 years, the effective interest rate stays at 6 percent because there is no prepayment penalty. As with points, the effective loan rate is higher the sooner the loan is repaid. If you think there is a good chance you will prepay your mortgage, try to get a loan with no prepayment penalty or at least a soft penalty that is waived after a few years or if you sell your home.

Table 7.1 Effective Interest Rate on a 30-Year Mortgage with a 6% Interest Rate and 5% Prepayment Penalty

Year Repaid	Effective Interest Rate (Percent)
1	10.78
2	8.33
3	7.51
4	7.11
5	6.87
10	6.39
20	6.15
30	6.00

Does Refinancing Pay?

A *Wall Street Journal* reporter had been tempted to refinance his 13.25 percent mortgage with a new 30-year mortgage at a 10 percent interest rate. He would have to pay nearly $4,000 in points, prepayment penalties, and other closing costs, but he figured that the lower monthly payments would be worth it. Then he realized that he only had 22 years left on his current mortgage, and that 22 years of his current mortgage payments would be less than 30 years of new payments. He would actually end up paying more money if he refinanced at a lower interest rate!

Do you see the total payments error again? His calculations simply add up the dollars paid, with no regard for the time value of money. One way to approach the problem is to consider refinancing with a 22-year mortgage, the same length as his current mortgage, with the same monthly payments as his current mortgage. The question then is whether he could borrow enough at these terms to pay off his old mortgage plus the $4,000 in closing costs. In fact, he could. He could have exactly the same monthly payments for the same number of years, pay the closing costs, and pocket nearly $10,000. This reporter was fooled by the total-payments error.

The Break-Even Refinancing Rate

We can use the reasoning in the previous example to answer this question: How low do interest rates have to fall to make refinancing profitable, despite points, prepayment penalties, and other costs? To keep the analysis straightforward, we again set the new loan so that:

1. The length of the new loan is equal to the time remaining on the original loan.
2. The amount borrowed with the new loan keeps the monthly payments the same.

The question then is whether the amount borrowed with the new loan pays off the balance on the old loan plus the prepayment penalty and other costs.

We will use a $100,000, 30-year mortgage at a 6 percent interest rate with $5,000 in points, penalties, and other refinancing costs as an example. Table 7.2 shows the break-even interest rates. If the new loan rate is less than the break-even rate, you can either reduce the monthly payments or keep the monthly payments the same and walk away with cash. If, for example, you refinance after 10 years at a 4 percent interest rate, you can either reduce the monthly payments from $600 to $537, or keep the monthly payments at $600 and put $10,327 in your pocket.

Table 7.2 Break-Even Interest Rate on a $100,000 Mortgage
with a 6% Interest Rate and $5,000 Refinancing Costs

Year Repaid	Break-Even Interest Rate (Percent)
1	5.54
5	5.46
10	5.29
20	4.08

Even with a seemingly stiff $5,000 in refinancing costs on a $100,000 mortgage, a 1 percent drop in interest rates is enough to make refinancing attractive in the first 10 years. As time passes and the number of years remaining at the old (high) interest rate dwindle, a bigger and bigger drop in interest rates is needed to make refinancing profitable.

No wonder a tidal wave of refinancings occurred as mortgage rates steadily fell from above 18 percent in the early 1980s to below 6 percent in the early 2000s. Some alert households refinanced mortgages on the same house three or four times. Every time they thought interest rates had bottomed, they refinanced. Then interest rates fell again and they refinanced again. Some inattentive households missed this great opportunity, either because they didn't notice that mortgage rates had dropped or because they didn't realize that a seemingly modest decline in interest rates can be worth thousands of dollars.

Wake Up, Little Susie

Susan and Ray Moore bought a home in June 2000 with a $235,000, 30-year mortgage at an 8.43 percent interest rate. In the spring of 2003, mortgage rates fell below 6 percent and they thought about refinancing. But it seemed like too much trouble, and what's a couple percent anyway? Finally, in June 2003, with mortgage rates at 5.43 percent, the Moores did their homework and refinanced.

What are 3 percentage-points worth? The monthly payments on their 8.43% mortgage were $1,795 and they had a balance of $229,108. Because this loan had 27 years remaining, let's assume they refinance with a 27-year loan and borrow just enough to repay the old loan and any refinancing costs. Here, the refinancing costs were under $1,000. So, they borrowed $230,000 for 27 years at 5.43%. Their monthly payments fell from $1,795 to $1,354, saving them $5,292 a year for 27 years. That got the Moore's attention!

They woke up and refinanced.

The Time Value of What?

Judy Lacy owns a home in West Palm Beach, Florida. In 1986, she received a letter from her bank that began:

We are very pleased to offer you the opportunity to save a minimum of $5,483.64 in future interest on your mortgage loan. Yes, you can save $5,483.64 in future interest by increasing your monthly payment by only $100.00 per month beginning in August. This extra $100.00 per month will also pay off your mortgage 3 years and 7 months early.

An enclosed analysis showed that Judy had an unpaid balance of $33,918.12 on a 7.25 percent loan, with 11 years and 11 months of $356 monthly payments remaining, and that,

With your present monthly payment of $356.00, your future interest paid over the next 11 years 11 months will be $16,740.16. By increasing your monthly payment by $100.00 per month, your future interest over the next 8 years 4 months will be $11,256.00. Your interest savings will be $5,483.64.

Judy was certainly tempted. She could afford the extra $100 a month and who could say no to saving more than $5,000? But then she started wondering why the bank was doing her a favor. They hadn't done her any favors before. And surely she wasn't the only one who received a letter like this. Why did the bank want their customers to pay off their mortgages early?

Then it all became clear. Mortgage rates were above 10 percent at the time. The bank was earning a 7.25 percent rate of return on Judy's mortgage when it could make new loans earning more than 10 percent. The bank wanted Judy (and all its other customers with low-interest loans) to pay off their loans so that the bank could relend the money at higher interest rates.

What about from Judy's perspective? Wasn't she saving $5,483.64 by paying off her loan early? Only if you ignore the time value of money. The bank's calculations add up the dollars paid over 11 years and 11 months with the dollars paid over 8 years and 4 months as if it doesn't matter when the dollars are paid. In one scenario, Judy pays more dollars, but over a longer period of time; in the other scenario, she pays fewer dollars but pays them sooner.

Which is better? The answer is simple if we apply the principle discussed in Chapter 5, "Debt Doesn't Have to be a Four-Letter Word": Judy will make money borrowing at a 7.25 percent interest rate if she can earn more than a 7.25 percent return on her investments. Because Judy could buy U. S. Treasury bonds earning well over 7.25 percent, she decided to keep her 7.25 percent mortgage. She resisted the temptation to write a nasty letter to her savings bank that began "How dare you try to trick me!"

Mental Accounting

When Jim Collins retired, he sold his home in Newport Beach, California, for $1.5 million and bought a home in Arizona for $500,000. His first thought was to pay cash for his new home because he wasn't working anymore and wouldn't have a monthly paycheck he could use to make his monthly mortgage payments. All his life, Jim had been doing mental accounting by putting money into different compartments. Salary is used to buy food and make mortgage payments; savings are used for vacations and his children's college expenses.

Another form of mental accounting is when somebody feels they can buy something because they saved money on something else. "I can buy a plasma television because I saved $2,000 on the car I bought." "We can go out for dinner tonight because I returned those clothes I bought yesterday." ("Gosh, honey, I wish you had bought and returned more clothes; then we could go out for dinner every night.")

Another kind of mental accounting is to spend whatever you earn. If I earn $3,000 a month, I can spend $3,000 a month. That is certainly better than spending $8,000 a month! But saving something for unexpected bills, your children's education, and retirement is even better. Sometimes, the only way people can save is if they put some money away as soon as they get paid: the first thing you spend your paycheck on is yourself, by writing a $100 check that is immediately mailed to your mutual fund.

Some people even use a direct deposit that comes out of each paycheck and goes into a mutual fund in order to force them to save.

Back to Jim Collins. If he pays $500,000 cash for his new home, he won't have to make any mortgage payments. However, if he does not pay cash, but instead invests the $500,000, the income from this investment might be more than enough to make his mortgage payments. Again, we are back to the principle discussed in Chapter 5: If Jim takes out a mortgage instead of paying cash, he will make a profit if he can earn a rate of return on his investments that is higher than his mortgage rate.

Jim's after-tax mortgage rate was about 4 percent and he decided he could earn a higher rate of return than that. He kept his money invested and took out a mortgage.

Selling Your Home Without Selling Your Home

Some people say their homes are not really an investment like stocks because they can always get cash by selling stocks, but they are not going to sell their home and live on the street. Actually, you can effectively sell part of your home and still live in it. With a home equity loan, you can borrow money at a relatively low (and often tax-deductible) interest rate and spend the money just as you might spend the proceeds from a stock sale. Suppose you have a $300,000 home with a $100,000 mortgage. Your equity is $200,000 because if you sell this home and pay off your mortgage, you will keep $200,000 (less expenses). You could choose to do this and perhaps move into a smaller home or a rental. But another alternative is to borrow $50,000, using your $200,000 equity as collateral for the loan. It's called a home equity loan because the equity in your home serves as collateral.

The home equity loan reduces your equity by $50,000—from $200,000 to $150,000. Now, if you sell your home for $300,000 and pay off your loans, you keep $150,000 instead of $200,000. Thus, you have effectively sold $50,000 of your home so that you can pay for your children's education or pay off your credit-card debt. Remember, your home is not an ATM. Don't use home equity loans to buy things you don't need. But sometimes a home equity loan is the cheapest way to pay for something you really do need.

Say No to Credit-Card Debt

One of the very best uses of home equity loans is to pay off credit-card debt. Credit cards are a great convenience for shopping, but a very expensive way to borrow money. With a credit card, you don't have to carry around cash and you can delay making the actual payment until the credit-card bill is due. However, if you don't pay the balance every month, the interest rate charged on credit-card balances is usually more than 10 percent and often more than 20 percent. And the interest isn't tax deductible. If you pay off $100 of credit-card debt that is being charged a 16 percent interest rate, you will save $16 in interest charges—in effect, investing $100 and getting a 16 percent return after taxes. The best investment many people can possibly make is to pay off their credit-card debt.

Households that don't have spare cash to pay off their credit-card might be able to use home equity loans, which usually have much lower interest rates and the interest is usually tax deductible (on up to $100,000 in home equity loans). Borrowing at a tax-deductible 8 percent to pay off a nondeductible 16 percent loan is very profitable.

The only caveat is that your home is collateral for a home equity loan. (That's why you get a favorable interest rate.) If you don't pay your credit-card debts on time, you will be charged more interest and your credit rating will take a hit. If you don't pay your home equity loan on time, your lender might foreclose and you might lose your home. So, don't take out a home equity loan thinking this will allow you to spend even more extravagantly. Take out a home equity loan because you want to pay off your credit-card debts immediately and use the lower interest rate to systematically pay off your home equity loan, too.

The very best strategy is to never use a credit card to borrow money. Credit cards are a wonderful convenience if you pay your bill each month, but very expensive if you don't.

One Way to Pay for College

Carlos Garcia and Emily James needed to borrow $100,000 to pay for their children's college education. They currently had a mortgage with a 5.375 percent interest rate that would be paid off in 11 years. They were trying to decide whether they should:
a. Increase the size of their mortgage by refinancing at a 6.75 percent interest rate, or
b. Keep their current mortgage and take out a home equity loan with an 8 percent interest rate.

The easiest way to compare apples to apples is to assume all the loans are amortized over the same 11-year period. Then you can simply see whether option (a) or (b) has the higher monthly payments. Option (b) is the winner. Carlos and Emily kept their 5.375 percent mortgage and used a home equity loan to pay for their children's college education.

The Bottom Line

1. Try to get a loan with no prepayment penalty or at least only a soft penalty that is waived after a few years or if you buy another home.
2. If you have many years left on your mortgage, refinancing can be profitable even if the new mortgage rate is only 1 percentage-point lower than your current rate.
3. Home equity loans let you borrow at a relatively low and usually tax-deductible rate to pay off credit-card debt, consumer-finance loans, and other high-interest, nondeductible loans.
4. Don't use home equity loans to buy things you don't need and can't really afford.
5. Before you take out a home equity loan, consider refinancing your current mortgage.

8

Remodeling

There are thousands of do-it-yourself stores spread across the nation: "You can try it. We can sell it!" Part of the appeal is that you can make your home just the way you want it. "Wouldn't it be great to have a cute little built-in bookcase behind this door? And a fountain with the soothing sound of running water? And rainbows and unicorns painted on the children's walls?" Part of the appeal is the satisfaction of a job well done, or at least done. "I'm so proud of you, honey." And part of the appeal is saving money. "Do you know what a contractor costs?"

When you are a renter, fixing up your landlord's property isn't sensible. But remodeling is one of the pains and pleasures of homeownership. When you own your home, you should fix your leaky windows, pipes, and roof because it will cost you more not to fix them. When you own your home, you can put in your dream kitchen, paint the walls any color you like, and make your bathroom bigger than your bedroom—whatever you want to do.

In this chapter, we will look at how you should evaluate remodeling projects.

Sunk Costs

When Valerie and Victor Nesterov bought their home, they loved the house but hated the backyard, which had taken years of abuse from three small children and two large dogs. The Nesterovs decided to turn an expanse of dead grass, bare dirt, and scraggly dandelions into a peaceful sanctuary of winding paths, beautiful flowers, and lovely patios. One 12' by 16' area posed a problem because it was next to a patio, was too big for a path, and did not get enough sun to grow anything they were interested in planting. Plus, the Nesterovs had already spent more than they had planned to spend on landscaping.

While visiting a home-supply store, they noticed some 16-by-24-inch cinder blocks with small diamond-shaped holes that could be used for growing ground cover. And, best of all, they were cheap! Unfortunately, their sprinkler pipes had already been laid and the ground cover would have to be watered by hand. Still, the blocks were cheap.

Figure 8.1 Cinder blocks for ground cover

So, the Nesterovs put in the cinder blocks and ground cover and tried to remember to water. They didn't remember often enough and the ground cover died. Now they had a 12-by-16-foot grid of cinder blocks with diamond-shaped holes—what they laughingly called "ankle breakers."

Clearly, these cinder blocks were a bad idea. But the Nesterovs had bought them and what else were they going to do with 72 ankle breakers? Victor figured that they would have to use them for at least 10 years to "get their money's worth," and that is what they did.

These ankle breakers are a *sunk cost* because the money was spent and cannot be unspent. Whether it was spent wisely or foolishly is unimportant. The ice-cream sundae you buy but can't finish is a sunk cost. The relevant question is not how much you paid for the ice cream, but whether you would be better off eating the rest of the ice cream or throwing it away. You shouldn't feel that you have to eat the rest of the sundae to get your money's worth.

The Nesterov's ankle-breakers are a sunk cost. The relevant question is not whether they should have bought the cinder blocks, but whether they should replace them with something more attractive and less dangerous. The relevant cost is not how much they paid for their 72 ankle breakers, but how much it would cost to put in something better. These ankle breakers are also an example of how being cheap is oftentimes a mistake. The Nesterovs would have been better off doing their landscaping right the first time, instead of doing it wrong before they did it right.

The same two lessons apply to all remodeling projects.

1. Remodeling makes sense if the benefits justify the additional cost.
2. Don't do something you will have to undo.

Does Remodeling Pay for Itself?

People often claim that a major remodeling project will pay for itself or more than pay for itself. "Spend $10,000 to upgrade your shower and the value of your home will increase by $15,000! Spend $50,000 to modernize your kitchen and the value of your home will increase by $75,000!" Maybe yes, maybe no. Buyers are certainly more likely to fall in love with a house with an upgraded shower and a modern kitchen—at least if their tastes match yours. And a remodeled house may well sell faster. But a house is not guaranteed to sell for a price high enough to cover the cost of a new shower and kitchen.

Appraisals and market prices are mostly based on comps, which are hardly affected by most remodeling projects. The main things that affect comps are location and square footage. Everything else is a dollar here, a dollar there. For example, let's look at the appraisal of a house in Westchester County, New York, that sold for $1 million in 2005. This house was in good condition, but had not had any remodeling for at least 20 years. One of the comps was a house that had been gutted and completely rebuilt. Everything in this comp house was brand new, top-of-the-line, and breathtakingly beautiful. The remodeling job cost well over $500,000 and the appraiser figured that it added $50,000 to the value of the home!

Table 8.1 shows part of the appraisal report. The "Subject" property is the property being appraised. "Sale #1" is a house that was sold recently and is being used to estimate the value of the subject property. The appraiser made several adjustments, but we show only four. The –$50,000 adjustment means that the subject property is worth $50,000 less than the Sale #1 property because it has not been remodeled and the Sale #1 property has been completely remodeled. A half million dollars spent on remodeling is only worth $50,000 to the appraiser.

Table 8.1 An Appraiser's Adjustments

Value Adjustments	Subject Description	Sale #1 Description	Dollar Adjustment
Remodeled	none	completely	–$50,000
Garage	2-car	4-car	–$6,000
Living area, square feet	2,562	3,913	–$101,500
Guest house	yes	no	$75,000

Sale #1 also has a 4-car garage, while the subject property has a 2-car garage; the appraiser figured the extra parking space for two cars was worth $6,000. The appraiser was consistent. Another property that was used as a comp had a 1-car garage and the appraiser figured that the difference between a 1-car garage and a 2-car garage was worth $3,000. The subject property has a permanent 10-by-12-foot storage shed with a concrete floor, double doors, and two windows. This shed wasn't worth a penny to the appraiser.

The subject property has a 1,000-square-foot guest house with a living room, bedroom, bathroom, and kitchen. The appraiser figured that this guest house was worth $75,000, which is $75 per square foot. Interestingly, the 1,351-square-foot difference in the size of the main residences was also valued at $75 per square foot: $75 × 1,351 = $101,325 rounded up to $101,500.

Why did all these properties sell for around $1 million? The three most important things in real estate are location, location,

location. These homes were in an expensive neighborhood, where homes were selling for around $1 million. The bigger houses sold for more, the smaller houses for less—plus or minus pocket change when we're talking about million-dollar homes.

Where do people get the idea that remodeling pays for itself? First, if you see an article in a magazine full of advertisements from the home-improvement industry, be skeptical, very skeptical. Second, think about how the authors of these studies typically come up with their numbers. Someone buys a house in 2001 for, say, $200,000, spends $20,000 on a remodeling project, and sells the house in 2004 for $230,000. Did the remodeling project increase the value of the house by $30,000? Well, maybe, if home prices haven't budged at all between 2001 and 2004. But what if home prices have gone up 15 percent during this period? We would expect a house that sold for $200,000 in 2001 to sell for $230,000 in 2004, even if the house had not been remodeled. In this situation, the remodeling project didn't increase the price at all.

The typical calculations you see in magazines and on the Internet don't ask, let alone answer, the relevant question, which is how much difference the project makes to the sale price. The only way to answer this question is to compare the prices of homes that have been remodeled with those that haven't. For example, these are two comparable homes: one with a new swimming pool, one with no pool. These are two comparable homes: one with an added bedroom, one without. And these are two comparable homes: one with a remodeled kitchen, one without. These comparisons are the kind made by real estate brokers and appraisers, and it is these comparisons that are the most relevant for estimating the effect of a remodeling project on your home's sale price.

Try to find a few realtors you can trust and ask them what they think your house will sell for. You can often find agents who are willing to prepare a detailed valuation based on comps because they think they might get your business. Their bottom line might be a little high because some realtors think they are more likely to get your business if they overestimate the sale price. If you have several valuations, you can gauge which are the most realistic.

Look over the valuations and see how your remodeling project might affect the sale price. For example, if houses with a swimming pool are worth $10,000 more than houses without pools, you can compare this to the cost of putting in a pool. After you've done your homework, ask these realtors to guesstimate how your remodeling project would affect the sale price. If they give you a crazy number, ask why the comps don't support this number. If they give you a plausible number, then you've got a reasonable answer to the relevant question: how much this remodeling project will increase the sale price of your home.

Remodel Sooner, Not Later

Steve and Tina Rhodes bought a house and raised a family in Armonk, New York. Their two daughters moved to northern California when they graduated from college. So, when Tim retired from IBM in 2004, Steve and Tina bought a home in Sunnyvale, California, so they could be closer to their daughters and their grandchildren. But after living in their Armonk house for 28 years, they figured they should try to make it perfect before trying to sell it. They spent the next 3 years doing a major remodel, including new floors and lighting and a modern kitchen with granite countertops and a breakfast bar. Yes, remodeling can take that long with architectural plans, architectural-commission approval, building permits, contractor bids, and stop-and-go construction.

This was almost certainly the wrong reason for remodeling. If Steve and Tina wanted a modern kitchen, they should have done it long ago so they could have enjoyed the kitchen for many years. By doing it right before they sold the house, they had to bear all the costs of living through the remodeling, while the new owners got all the benefits of having a new kitchen. The sale price did not increase enough to cover the cost of remodeling and, in the meantime, the Rhodes paid tens of thousands of dollars in mortgage payments and property taxes on an empty house in Sunnyvale.

Make It Bigger, Not Better

A house's square footage is crucial for comps. You can therefore feel pretty confident that a remodeling project that increases the size of your house will increase the estimated value of your home —and you can get a pretty good idea of what the impact will be.

In the Westchester County example in Table 8.1, the appraiser valued a 1,000-square-foot guest house at $75 per square foot and also valued the difference in the size of the main residences at $75 per square foot. The specific dollars-per-square-foot numbers will vary from place to place, presumably depending on local construction costs. If you can increase the size of your house at a cost of $75 per square foot, and realtors and appraisers will put a value of $75 per square foot on the size of your house, then you can feel pretty confident that the comp value of your house will increase by the cost of the expansion. If this expansion also makes your home more livable, then remodeling is clearly appealing. If, on the other hand, construction costs are $200 per square foot, you are going to need a lot more than a higher sale price to justify remodeling.

You also saw in the Westchester County example that a 1-car difference in the size of the garage was worth $3,000 to the appraiser. You might not like the number, but at least you can be pretty sure this number will show up in appraisals, and you can compare this number to the construction cost. More generally, if you make your home bigger, you can get a reasonable estimate of the effect on the appraised value of your home.

Home improvements like upgraded windows, refinished floors, or a new shower are harder to quantify. If you are making it better, not bigger, most of your justification for remodeling has to be that it improves your lifestyle enough to make it worth the cost.

What's a Remodeling Project Really Worth?

You can probably guess how we think a remodeling project ought to be evaluated. If you are about to sell your home, you can do lots of inexpensive, cosmetic things to make your home more appealing. Put some pretty flowers in the front yard to enhance the curb appeal; get the spiderwebs off the front porch; have your garage sale before you sell the house, not after. Some repairs and remodeling are necessary for curb appeal, like replacing the battered mailbox; fixing the rotten front steps; and putting the front door back on its hinges.

It can also pay to rejuvenate a genuine fixer-upper. Most home buyers like to see "move-in condition" (real estate code for a house that doesn't need any work) instead of "handyman's special" (real estate code for a house that has been trashed). A trashed house is hard to sell to anyone other than a trash collector —an energetic person who plans to buy it cheap, fix it up, sell it, and move on to the next reclamation project. A renovation can be profitable for professionals, but is a nightmare for amateurs.

Other than curb-appeal projects and complete makeovers of trashed homes, we are skeptical about remodeling right before a sale. Planning and overseeing a major remodeling project sucks up your time and the construction thoroughly disrupts your life. The building permits, the noise, the sawdust, the no-shows, the botched work. Remodeling just isn't worth the headaches. Let the buyer deal with it.

Plus, who says the buyer will appreciate the hell you went through? We know a family that completely relandscaped their backyard, using a professional landscape architect to design a beautiful layout of winding paths through beds of eye-catching flowers; the buyers tore it all out and put in an asphalt playground and grass soccer field. We know a family that put in new carpet throughout their house; the buyers tore it up and refinished the wood floors. We know a family that repainted the interior of their house with Craftsman colors selected by a professional designer; the buyers repainted everything Navajo White.

Our advice is to be cautious—very cautious—about remodeling to increase your home's sale price. Think instead of remodeling to improve your lifestyle. The buyers who put in the asphalt playground and soccer field wanted a yard their children could play in. The buyers who tore up the carpet and refinished the wood floors were concerned about allergies. The buyers who repainted everything Navajo White thought the Craftsman colors were bizarre. These reasons are exactly the right ones for remodeling. Do it (and the sooner the better) if the improvement in your lifestyle is well worth the cost; otherwise, don't.

Sometimes you can get a rough estimate of a remodeling project's home dividends. Consider, for example, a swimming pool. A house's home dividends depend on the rental savings. In the same way, imagine that you can rent a swimming pool. And you can sort of rent a pool by joining a club that has a swimming pool. Of course, that is not nearly as convenient or as much fun as having your own private pool in your backyard. So try to imagine that you can rent a pool in your backyard and think about how much you would pay every year for this.

Suppose it costs $200 per month to join a club with a pool (and you wouldn't use any facilities other than the pool). Suppose also that you are willing to pay an extra $200 per month if the pool is in your backyard. If the pool is in your backyard, you are going to have to take care of it, and maybe that's $100 per month. Include some additional expenses for water and electricity, plus the increase in your homeowner's insurance premiums. If you borrow money to pay for the pool, that is another expense. All these numbers will increase over time and a pool needs major repairs every once in a while. On the other hand, a pool might increase the sale price of your home. Home dividend calculations can take all these factors into account. If the home dividends look good, then a pool is financially attractive; otherwise, join a club.

Our point is that you should consider two very distinct things when you are mulling over a remodeling project.

1. *How much will the project improve your lifestyle?* You can try to value the lifestyle improvement by estimating what you are hypothetically willing to pay to rent a swimming pool, an additional bedroom, or a modernized kitchen.

2. *How much will the project increase your home's sale price?* You can try to estimate the increased market price by looking at comps for homes with and without the project you are considering; for example, with and without a swimming pool, or with and without an additional bedroom.

If you aren't planning to sell your home anytime soon, then the first consideration (an improved lifestyle) is all that matters. If you are planning to sell your home in a few years, the second consideration is important, too.

Leaky Windows

Jim and Leslie Brown were at a neighborhood block party and the conversation turned from kids' soccer games to electricity bills. The Browns have electric heat and air conditioning and their electric bills average $300 a month in the winter and $500 a month in the summer—more than double their neighbor's bills. Why? Their heater and air conditioner are newer than their neighbors' equipment and presumably more efficient. They set their thermostat lower than their neighbors do in the winter and higher than their neighbors do in the summer. So the problem isn't that they aren't trying to economize. Their house is a lot older than their neighbors' houses, but the Browns have thick plaster walls and a 100-year-old oak tree that shades the house in the summer.

Then Leslie remembered the rattling windows. The Browns had old-fashioned, double-hung, single-pane windows that are far from airtight. Their windows rattle when the wind blows. And the Browns move their beds and chairs away from the windows in the winter because of the cold air leaking through the windows.

So, the Browns considered replacing all the leaky windows in their house with airtight windows. They found a highly recommended handyman and got a quote of $19,000 for replacing 27 windows. Should they do it?

They compared the tangible benefits with the cost. They estimated that the new windows would reduce their electric bill by about $2,000 a year. Their savings will probably go up over time as electricity costs increase, but they decided to be conservative and stick with $2,000 a year. They expected to live in this house for at least another 10 years and they assumed that their sale price would be $10,000 higher because the buyers would appreciate the more attractive and energy-efficient windows. They used a financial calculator and found that, with a 6 percent after-tax return, the value of the $2,000 annual savings on their electric bills and the $10,000 higher sale price was $20,300, just enough to justify putting in the new windows.

They realized that their assumptions were generally conservative. The value of the benefits would be $2,000 to $4,000 higher if they happen to stay in the house for another 15 years instead of 10 years, or if their electric-bill savings increase by 3 percent a year instead of remaining constant. Plus, they hadn't taken into account any benefit they might derive from having more beautiful windows or putting their beds and chairs next to windows. They decided to put in new windows and they have been very happy with that decision.

I'd Rather Do It Myself

If, like us, your favorite home-repair tools are spackle and duct tape, you're probably better off not doing any serious repairs or remodeling on your own. We would probably do more damage than good, and maybe you're the same way, too. Unless it is your profession, leave it to the professionals.

When people boast that they saved hundreds or even thousands of dollars on a home repair or remodeling project, they are valuing their own time at nothing an hour and assuming that a professional job done well is no better than an amateur job done poorly. They have the same mindset as people who save a few dollars by buying a project from IKEA that takes all weekend to assemble. (Been there, done that.)

Generally, we recommend that you pay a professional to do a professional job. However, we have two exceptions to this rule.

1. You are a professional and you know what you are doing.
2. Home repairs and improvements are a hobby. You are doing it because it is fun and you enjoy it, in the same way that people have backyard vegetable gardens that produce heirloom tomatoes at a cost of $5 apiece. (We have one of these gardens.)

Another useful guideline is, "Don't be cheap!" We are not recommending that you be extravagant. What we mean is that if you are going to do a remodeling project that you will live with for a long time (and that should be your plan), don't do something cheap and cheesy that you will regret forever. Remember those ankle breakers? Smart carpenters "measure twice, cut once" to avoid mistakes. The same principle applies to remodeling projects. It is expensive to do a project and then do it over again. Do it right the first time.

Bob Tucker is a handyman wannabe who added a fourth bedroom to his house. Because his house is on a slope, Bob put the ceiling for this extra bedroom below the ceiling for the rest of the house, and put the bedroom floor below the floor for the rest of the house—which meant that anyone entering the new bedroom had to duck and step down. When he was selling his house, most of the buyers who came to see the property did not want to duck and step down; instead, they headed for the front door. The first remodeling project for the family that finally bought this house was to bulldoze the fourth bedroom.

It is a good sign if you call a contractor recommended by two friends and the contractor says he is booked for the next 15 months. It is a bad sign if a contractor says he can start today. It's a really bad sign if a someone knocks on your door and says that he is doing some work in the neighborhood and wonders if he can do some work for you, too.

Paying By the Job or By the Hour?

Paying by the hour seems fairer, but paying by the job is safer. It might be our imagination but it seems that workers paid by the hour tend to work at a more leisurely pace than do workers paid by the job. You certainly don't want workers to be fast and sloppy, but workers who are paid by the hour seem to spend a lot of time talking to each other and talking on their cell phones.

The Platts once made the mistake of paying a handyman by the hour. The handyman brought along two helpers who were also paid by the hour. When they knew the Platts were watching, all three would assume various work positions, though sometimes doing nothing more than pushing dust around with a broom or bending over a tool chest. When the workers didn't think the

Platts were paying attention, one person was almost always watching the other two, and sometimes two persons were watching the third. Three workers were definitely not three times as productive as one.

The Big Job in Waltham

After Jennifer and John Sykes bought a home in Watertown, Massachusetts, they called three general contractors for bids on adding a bedroom and remodeling a bathroom. They chose Joe Clark, who was very personable and submitted the lowest bid. Then the trouble started. Joe Clark is one of those contractors who never turns down a job and often has more jobs than he can handle. Joe doesn't do the actual work; he just hires subcontractors (subs) and, in theory, coordinates and supervises their work. In practice, his subs are overworked with all the jobs Joe has taken. The subs say they will be at a dozen different places each day, but make it to perhaps three or four. When the subs do show up, they often work for an hour or so and then leave, saying that they have to get to their "big job" in Waltham, Newton, or Belmont. It is very inefficient for them to spend hours each day driving between multiple jobs, but that's one of the costs of overbooking.

And that low price? Jennifer and John were prudent enough to sign a contract that spelled out exactly what work was to be done. Or at least that is what they thought they signed. As the project wound down, they were in for some nasty surprises. The subs put unfinished cabinets in the bathroom and refused to finish them, saying "That's not in the contract." The subs didn't paint the interior or exterior walls of the bedroom that they added: "That's not in the contract."

When the subs put new flooring in the bathroom, they removed the baseboard that covers where the wall and floor meet. During the baseboard removal, the finish was marred and nail holes were left in the baseboard. Joe's subs did not repair or remount the baseboard: "That's not in the contract." Jennifer told Joe Clark that if the subs didn't repair the damaged baseboard and remount it, she would leave it on the floor and tell everyone who visited their house that this was how Joe Clark worked. Joe finally agreed to redo the baseboard, but he wouldn't finish the cabinets or paint the walls.

It is really, really hard to spell out every single detail in a remodeling job. The best protection is to choose someone who is highly recommended by people you trust.

The Bottom Line

1. Don't remodel until you've thought seriously about the costs and benefits.
2. Remodeling increases the sale price most reliably if it increases your home's square footage.
3. Improving your lifestyle is usually more important than increasing the sale price.
4. If you are going to remodel, do it sooner rather than later so that you can enjoy it for many years.
5. Do it right the first time so you don't have to redo it.
6. Unless it is your profession, hire a professional.

Rental Properties and Vacation Homes

Once you understand that the investment value of a home depends on the home dividend, then you also know how to value rental properties and vacation homes—indeed, how to value any investment. The value of an investment depends on the income you get from the investment. Buy a rental property or a vacation home for the income, not because you think the price will increase rapidly.

You Paid Landlords; Now You Are a Landlord

You've seen that the income from your home comes from the rent savings. If the rent savings are large enough to make your home a profitable investment, then it would appear that buying a home and renting it to someone else will also be a profitable investment. This general idea is correct but a few details can complicate matters.

One detail is that when you buy a home and live in it, you save rent every single month. But if you buy a home and rent it out, you only collect rent if you have tenants. If there is a gap between when one tenant moves out and the next tenant moves in, you will lose rent while the home is vacant. You will also lose rent if tenants refuse to pay and it takes a while to evict them.

Your maintenance expenses might also increase. If you live in your own home and have a leaky faucet, you can just slip in a new washer. If you are a landlord and the property is not close by, you might have to pay a plumber $75 to slip in the new washer. Also, people who own the home they live in are more likely to take good care of it. People living in a stranger's home are more likely to be careless or destructive. Thus your maintenance expenses are likely to be much larger if you rent a home to someone else than if you live in it yourself. Finally, the tax rules are different for owner-occupied homes than for rental properties.

Adverse Selection

Adverse selection occurs when high-risk people take advantage of deals intended for low-risk people. For example, if life insurance companies cannot distinguish those in poor health from those in good health, then it must offer the same premium to both. Those in poor health are more likely to buy such policies and make claims, which reduces the insurance company's profits.

In the real estate market, an adverse-selection problem arises if people choose to rent because they believe that they are likely to lose their job, are not handy around the home, are accident prone, or have unruly children and pets. We are not saying that these are universal traits, only that these characteristics might be more prevalent among renters. If they are more prevalent, then landlords might find themselves with tenants who are unemployed klutzes with destructive children and pets.

Moral Hazard

Economists say there is a *moral hazard* problem when a person behaves differently if someone else is paying the bills. For example, a person might be less careful about locking doors if he has theft insurance; a person might be less concerned about the cost of medical tests if the insurance company pays for the tests.

In extreme cases, unscrupulous people crash insured automobiles and burn down insured buildings, as illustrated by the following joke. Two friends meet each other unexpectedly at a European resort. The first person explains that he bought a warehouse and it burned down; he is using the insurance proceeds to pay for his vacation. The second person responds that he bought some property that was destroyed in a flood and that he, too, is spending the insurance money on a vacation. "Gee," the first person asks, "How do you start a flood?"

Deliberately causing damage to collect insurance is illegal. But it is not illegal to be less careful. In the real estate market, it seems self-evident that most people will take better care of a home if they own it than if they rent it. The McCully family learned this lesson the hard way. They rented out their Vermont home while they spent a year in Scotland with relatives. Their tenants piled the mattresses in the front yard so that their children could jump off the roof, roasted marshmallows around a campfire on the living-room floor, and ripped a bathroom sink out of the wall and took it with them when they moved out. Would these tenants have done any of these things to their own home?

That story is real. The next is a joke (I hope). Jack lives in New Hampshire and his heating bills have skyrocketed. Seeing all the trees around him, he realizes that he can heat his home by burning logs. One day, he tells his friend Mack to come over and bring an ax and a chain saw. Jack found an old oil drum at the town dump and wants to get it down in the basement. The drum won't fit through the cellar door, so Jack uses the ax to cut down some posts and widen the opening. Once the drum is in the basement, the plan is to burn logs in the drum and let the heat rise to warm the house. The next problem is how to get the heat from the basement into the house. No problem. Jack also found an old 3-foot-square heating grate at the dump. He walks into the living room, traces an outline of the grate on the wooden floor, and then uses the chain saw to cut a slightly smaller hole that the grate can rest on. He nails the grate in place with some two-by-fours. Problem solved. No one will fall through the hole in the floor and the heat from the burning logs in the oil drum will warm the house nicely. Mack admires Jack's ingenuity, but asks what the insurance company will think of this heating system. Jack replies, "Insurance? That's the owner's problem!"

Long-Distance Landlords

We live in southern California, where home prices are—to the naked eye—kind of high. When we look at other parts of the country, we often find homes that look like great investments. As in the Fishers, Indiana, example earlier in this book, home prices are so low relative to the home dividend that buying a home to live in has an estimated after-tax return that is well over 10 percent.

This doesn't seem to be a temporary aberration. We have looked at 23 years of data and found homes to be attractively priced for most of these years in many parts of the heartland. For example, in the Indianapolis area, homes were a good investment 23 years ago and have become an even better investment over time. Rising rents and falling interest rates have increased home dividends greatly, while home prices have risen by a leisurely 2.2 percent a year.

If you think that this modest 2.2 percent price appreciation makes Indianapolis homes a poor investment, remember that price appreciation is generally less important than the home dividends. What makes Indianapolis homes a great investment is the terrific home dividends. The average Indianapolis home that we looked at in 2005 cost $14,000 a year to rent but could be bought for only $146,000. People who are going to live in Indianapolis for a while can almost surely look forward to a very rewarding return from buying a home there.

Economists tell the story of two finance professors walking down the street when one spots a $100 bill on the sidewalk. As he bends to pick it up, the other says, "Don't bother; if it were real, someone would have picked it up by now." Finance professors are fond of saying that the stock market doesn't leave $100 bills lying on the sidewalk, meaning that if there was an easy way to make money in the stock market, someone would have figured it out by now. Home prices in the heartland suggest that the real estate market is leaving suitcases full of $100 bills on the sidewalk.

When we saw these suitcases, we looked into becoming long-distance landlords, buying single-family homes in Indianapolis, Atlanta, Dallas, and many other parts of the country and renting them to local residents. But the closer we looked, the less attractive this appeared. We would have to research the neighborhoods and fly out to look at the homes before buying them. We would need to pay someone to screen prospective tenants and keep an eye on the houses. We would have to pay someone to do home repairs. (We can't fly to Indianapolis to replace a washer!) Property-management companies will take care of a lot of the details, but their fees are typically 5 to 10 percent of the rent. We would also need to deal with vacancies, unpaid rent, and damage to the property. The costs just kept piling up. And the number of $100 bills in the suitcases kept getting smaller and smaller.

The conclusion we came to is that the housing market can be very inefficient because it is very difficult to profit from these inefficiencies.

Ah, the Tax Code

If you own your own home, you get lots of tax breaks that landlords do not get. Most importantly, the rent a landlord receives is taxable income, but you don't pay taxes on the rent you save by living in your own home. Expenses are also handled differently, but the proverbial bottom line is that the prospective after-tax income is generally lower when buying a home to rent than when buying the same home to live in.

Fishers, Indiana, Again

In Chapter 3, "Now is a Good Time to Own a Home," we looked at the 3-bedroom, 3-bath house that the Nelsons purchased in Fishers, Indiana, (a suburb of Indianapolis) in 2005. They paid $135,000 for this house and could have rented a very similar house for $1,250 a month ($15,000 a year). Table 9.1 shows that if the Nelsons live in this home, their estimated home dividend in the first year is $5,622.

Table 9.1 First-Year, After-Tax Home Dividend for an Owner-Occupied Home in Fishers, Indiana

Income and Expenses	Dollar Amount
Rent savings	$15,000
Mortgage payment	–$7,522
Property tax	–$2,619
Tax savings	$2,447
Insurance	–$334
Utilities	$0
Maintenance	–$1,350
Home dividend	$5,622

The Nelsons bought this home to live in, but let's see what the home dividend would have been if they had rented this home to someone else for $15,000 a year. First, we have to determine the taxes on their rental income. Table 9.2 estimates their taxable income. (Appendix B, "A Rental Home in Fishers, Indiana," explains the details.)There is, in fact, a loss for tax purposes.

Table 9.2 First-Year Taxable Income for a
Rental Home in Fishers, Indiana

Income and Expenses	Dollar Amount
Rental income	$15,000
Interest portion of mortgage payment	−$6,120
Property tax	−$3,564
Insurance	−$612
Utilities	$0
Maintenance	−$1,350
Depreciation	−$3,682
Taxable income	−$328

People who are not real estate professionals typically cannot deduct rental losses against other income because the rental property would then be a tax shelter rather than a real business. (There is a "small-investor" exception because the law is intended to curtail the use of rental properties as tax shelters by wealthy persons.)

The Nelsons are not real estate professionals and do not qualify for the small-investor exception. They consequently cannot deduct this loss from their taxable income.

Now that we have the Nelson's tax bill (zero), we can calculate their home dividend. Table 9.3 compares the first-year home dividend if the Nelsons live in this home with the home dividend if they rent it to someone else. Notice two things. First, as landlords, their home dividend is positive even though they have a loss for tax purposes. This is one reason why the government is concerned about the use of rental properties as tax shelters. Second, the home dividend is much smaller for the Nelsons if they rent the home out than if they live in their home.

Table 9.3 Comparison of First-Year Home Dividend for a
Home That Is Owner-Occupied or Rented to Someone Else

	Owner-Occupier	Landlord
Rent savings or income	$15,000	$15,000
Mortgage payment	–$7,522	–$7,522
Property tax	–$2,619	–$3,564
Tax savings or payment	$2,447	$0
Insurance	–$334	–$612
Utilities	$0	$0
Maintenance	–$1,350	–$1,350
Home dividend	$5,622	$1,952

The two biggest factors that cut into their home dividend
when the Nelsons rent the home out are:

1. Indiana, like many states, has lower property taxes for
   owner-occupied homes than for rental properties.
2. Landlords do not receive a tax saving from mortgage
   interest and property taxes because these must be used
   (together with depreciation and other expenses) to avoid
   paying taxes on the rental income. Owner occupiers do not
   have to do this because their rental savings are not
   considered taxable income. They can consequently use
   mortgage interest and property taxes to reduce the taxes
   they pay on their other income.

The landlord numbers in Table 9.3 might be too optimistic. We
initially assumed that the maintenance expenses are $1,350 (1
percent of the value of the property) regardless of whether the
Nelsons live in the home or rent it out. We used the same
maintenance expense for each case because we wanted to focus on
how the Nelson's home dividend is affected by the different tax
rules for owner-occupied homes and rental properties.

In practice, the Nelson's maintenance costs are probably going
to be higher if the home is rented, for the reasons discussed earlier.
So, let's increase the maintenance expense from 1 percent to 2
percent; that is, from $1,350 to $2,700. Table 9.4 shows that the net

home dividend falls from \$1,952 to \$602. The home dividend is almost gone!

Table 9.4 A Rental Home in Fishers, Indiana, Loses Some of Its Luster with Higher Maintenance Expenses

Income and Expenses	Dollar Amount
Rental income	\$15,000
Mortgage payment	−\$7,522
Property tax	−\$3,564
Taxes	\$0
Insurance	−\$612
Utilities	\$0
Maintenance	−\$2,700
Taxable income	\$602

If we allow for slightly higher maintenance expenses and periods of time when the home is vacant and not bringing in rental income, the home dividend can turn negative. This home might still be attractive as a rental property because we are only looking at the first-year home dividend, and the home dividend is likely to improve over time as the rent increases and mortgage payments do not. Our point is simply that the home dividend can be a lot lower for a rental property than for an owner-occupied home.

There are three lessons. First, complicated tax laws and problematic tenants will be challenging. Second, just like the home you live in, the investment value of a rental property depends on the home dividend. Don't buy a rental property hoping that it will appreciate; do buy a rental property because the home dividend justifies the price. Third, a home can look much more financially attractive to an owner-occupier than to a landlord. This is why homes in places like Fishers, Indiana, are great for people like the Nelsons who are looking for a home to live in and yet not be snapped up by investors looking for suitcases full of \$100 bills.

If I Bought It, It Must be Worth the Price I Paid

George and Mary Parker live in Naples, Florida, a small city on the southeastern coast of Florida. The Naples beach has been voted the best beach in the United States, and the town itself boasts that it has more golf courses, millionaires, and CEOs per capita than any other city in the country. After the dot-com stock-market crash, the Parkers sold all their stocks and decided to invest in real estate by buying small Naples homes in older neighborhoods on the wrong side of the highway—away from the beach.

Home prices in Naples more than doubled between 2001 and 2005 and, along the way, the Parkers made a lot of money flipping homes. They bought their first Naples investment property in 2001 for $180,000, with a $30,000 down payment and a $150,000 mortgage. They made some cosmetic repairs and sold it nine months later for $210,000. They used the profits from this sale to buy two similar homes, which they again sold in less than a year. By 2005, they owned 13 Naples homes, all very much like the first home they bought in 2001. In fact, they bought one home in 2002, sold it in 2003, and bought it back again in 2005 for twice what they had paid in 2002. Sometimes they would rent these homes to help make the mortgage payments; other times, they flipped a home before they had time to find a renter.

The Naples housing market weakened in 2006 and the easy flipping ended. The Parkers' rental income wasn't covering their mortgage payments and buyers weren't lining up to buy homes. The Parkers tried to sell one home through a real estate auction, but the highest bid was 30 percent less than the price they had paid in 2005. The Parkers refused to accept this bid or to consider the possibility that they had paid too much for these homes. George argued that the prices they paid were okay because the appraisers always valued these homes at close to the purchase price.

Where did the appraisers' numbers come from? From comps, of course. The house they bought in 2002 and repurchased in 2005 was appraised at $220,000 in 2002 and at $450,000 in 2005 because that's what similar houses were selling for in 2002 and 2005. These appraisals don't mean that the house was actually worth $220,000 in 2002 and $450,000 in 2005, only that these were the market prices in these years. A Beanie Baby isn't worth $500 because some fool paid $500 for it. A dot-com stock isn't worth $200 because some fool paid $200 for it. A Naples rental property isn't worth $450,000 because the Parkers paid $450,000 for it. A rental property isn't worth $450,000 unless it generates enough rental income to justify that price. The Parker's rental properties did not.

A Home with Two Rentals

The Royers bought a home in the Chicago suburbs. One of the things they like about this home is that it is close to work and good schools. Another is that the house is on a triple lot with a 2,500-square-foot, 4-bedroom, 3-bath main house and two smaller 1,000-square-foot, 1-bedroom, 1-bath houses that can be used as guest houses, offices, or rental properties. If rented out, the rent from these two guest houses would cover more than half of their mortgage payments on the entire property. The total home dividend from the main house and the two guest houses was large and would get even larger over time.

The Royers were able to buy this home for what they considered a low price because the sellers focused on the comps for the main house and assigned little value to the guest houses. The appraiser did the same. He valued the main house at $500,000 ($200 per square foot) and valued each of the guest houses at $30,000 ($30 per square foot), with no consideration of the income potential. The Royers bought the property for $560,000 and considered it a bargain because of the great home dividend.

After living in this house for five years, the Royers got a can't-pass-this-up job offer a thousand miles away. They decided to sell their house privately—in part, to save on commissions and, in part, because they knew from experience that real estate agents would be fixated on comps for the main house and greatly underestimate the value of the rental properties. They ran the numbers again with updated values and used these numbers to price their house and to try to persuade potential buyers how valuable the rentals were. It paid off. They found buyers who, like the Royers, could appreciate what their property was really worth.

Those Darn Taxes

Marie and Ray Lopez bought a home in northern California in 1999 for $450,000. They liked the house, but the neighborhood turned out to be a disappointment. By 2005, the Lopezes had two young children (ages 3 and 6) and all of their neighbors were either retired or young professionals with no children. The yards are very clean—okay, immaculate—and the streets are very quiet. Does anyone live here? Most of the neighbors leave for work early in the morning and return in the evening. The rest stay indoors and watch television (or whatever it is that retired people do). The only signs of life are the gardeners' lawnmowers and leaf blowers as they mow and blow to keep everything immaculate. In the Lopez's words, the neighborhood is "sterile."

In 2005, they found another home for sale in the same city but in a very different neighborhood. This home was within walking distance to an elementary school, a park, restaurants, a world-class bakery, and a neighborhood grocery store. Best of all, bicycles were in the neighbors' driveways. Their offer on this new house was accepted. Now they had to decide what to do with their old house. They estimated that they could sell their old home for $900,000, which was a lot better return than they had gotten in the stock market. If this home was such a great investment, maybe they should rent it out for a few years before selling it.

They did some calculations and found that they could expect an okay home dividend from renting their old house—not breathtaking, but okay. The problem was that the value of their old home had increased by $450,000. If they sold it now, they wouldn't have to pay a capital gains tax on their $450,000 profit because they would qualify for the $500,000 capital gains exclusion (for homes that are the primary residence for at least two of the preceding five years). If, however, they rented it out for more than three years, they would lose the capital gains exclusion. The $500,000 capital gains exclusion with a 15 percent capital gains tax was worth $75,000. If they factored in this cost, the numbers didn't work anymore. The returns went from okay to no way.

The only way the numbers worked was if they avoided the capital gains tax by never selling the house, which was out of the question for a variety of reasons. The capital gains tax tipped the balance, and they sold their old house.

The Investment Value of a Vacation Home

Most people like to go on vacation to mountain cabins, beach houses, ski resorts, and amusement parks. The world is full of leisure destinations. Some prefer the novelty of going somewhere different every year. The Spencers went to Orlando in 2002, Banff in 2003, London in 2004, Tuscany in 2005, Cancun in 2006, and Maui in 2007. Some want to go somewhere different every day— the legendary cross-country road trip that begins with joyful songs and ends with wornout travelers and a car full of junk-food wrappers. "No, we haven't got time to see the world's largest stuffed possum; we have to be in Gallup by sundown. Yes, you can have another bag of GummySweets if you stop whining. No, I didn't know this motel doesn't have air conditioning."

Some people go back to the same place year after year. The Barbers spend two weeks every Christmas in the same condominium in Hawaii. The Noones spend 3 weeks every summer at a camp in the Pocono Mountains in northeastern Pennsylvania. The Palmers live and work in Boston, Massachusetts, but have a vacation home in nearby Chatham, on the elbow of Cape Cod.

If you do go back to the same vacation place year after year, it might be cheaper to buy a vacation home than to rent one every year, especially if you can rent it out when you aren't staying there. In principle, valuing a vacation home is like valuing an owner-occupied home and valuing a rental property, because a vacation home is a little bit of both. In practice, the calculations can be tricky because tax laws have special provisions that apply to vacation homes.

For example, the number of days that you (or your family or friends) use the home for personal purposes determines whether the vacation home meets the criteria for being classified as a personal residence or as a rental property. If you use the home for personal purposes for more than 14 days in a year or 10 percent of the rental days, whichever is greater, then the home is considered a personal residence. For example, if you rent the home out for 90 days, you need to stay in it for at least 15 days; if you rent the home out for 180 days, you need to stay in it for at least 19 days.

If your vacation home fits into the personal-residence category, then you don't need to report or pay taxes on any rental income you receive unless the home is rented for more than 14 days during the year. You simply deduct the property taxes and interest (on up to $1 million of mortgage debt on two personal residences plus $100,000 in home equity loans). If the home is rented for more than 14 days, then you need to report the rental income and allocate your expenses (including mortgage interest and property taxes) on the vacation home between its personal use and rental use. The rules are complicated, but the typical effect is to reduce the net taxable rental income to zero.

If your vacation home falls into the rental-property category, then you are not allowed to deduct the personal-use portion of your mortgage interest and the rules for allocating expenses are also a bit different from the rules for a personal residence. As we said, the rules are complicated and you will probably need assistance from an accountant or other experienced professional.

Still, in principle, one can figure out the home dividend (including both the rental savings for your personal use and the rental income for the rental use) the same way you would determine the home dividend for a home that was always owner-occupied or for a home that was always used as a rental property.

The Bi-Coastal Renkens

Herb and Doris Renken are professors in Davis, California, where Herb teaches English and Doris teaches Physics from early September to early May. The other four months of the year, they live in a 4-bedroom, 3-bath house on 7.5 acres of forest land with 650 feet of pond frontage in Brewster, Massachusetts.

Because they own their vacation home, Herb and Doris can leave pretty much everything they need for the summer in their Brewster home. Herb has a sailboat and two canoes; Doris has everything she needs for quilting. Herb has a professionally laid out horseshoe pit. Doris has a vegetable garden with rich soil built up from decades of composting. Herb has his favorite spots for clamming. Doris has her favorite spots for gathering wild blueberries. They both have all the clothing and household goods they need for the summer. And they have long-established friendships in Brewster with year-rounders and summer vacationers who return yearly.

What is the home dividend for this vacation home? Let's start with the four months they live there. For the prime vacation weeks, they would have to pay about $4,000 a week to rent a home like this, not counting the value they place on having all their personal items waiting for them every May. In late spring and late summer, the rents might be half this amount. During the eight months of the year when they are living in California, they rent their Brewster home for $1,000 a month to people that they know will take care of the property.

After taking into account the mortgage payments and other expenses, they estimated the home dividend to be very attractive. Not only do they vacation in paradise, they have a great investment, too.

The Bottom Line

1. Buy a rental property for the home dividend, not because you think the price will increase rapidly.
2. Be prepared for complicated tax laws and problematic tenants.
3. Taxes and tenants usually make rental properties less profitable than buying a home to live in.
4. If you vacation in the same place often, consider buying a vacation home.
5. The investment value of a vacation home depends on the home dividend—the rent you save and any rental income minus the mortgage and other expenses.

10

Letting Your Home Take Care of You

You will spend much of your life taking care of your home. Will a time come when your home takes care of you? Of course, your home will always take care of you physically and emotionally by giving you a familiar and comfortable place to eat, play, and rest; and a place that you can be proud of owning, maintaining, and improving. But what about financially? The answer is yes, Your home is very much like a retirement account that can support you during retirement.

HRAs

A traditional *Individual Retirement Account (IRA)* is a tax-deferred plan: you don't pay taxes on the income you put into the IRA or on any profits earned while the money is inside the plan, but you pay taxes when you take your money out. For example, suppose you put $2,000 of your income into an IRA and it quadruples to $8,000 in 24 years (about a 6 percent annual return). You don't pay income taxes on the $2,000 that you put in and you don't pay taxes each year on your profits, but you do pay taxes on the $8,000 when you take your money out. If you are in the same tax bracket when you put the money in and when you take it out, this tax deferral turns your IRA into a tax shelter in that if you earn a 6 percent annual return inside your IRA, the effective after-tax rate of return is 6 percent. This same principle applies to a variety of tax-deferred retirement plans, including 401(k) and 403(b) plans.

Table 10.1 shows that a *Roth IRA* works a bit differently, but has similar results. You pay taxes on your income before you put it into the plan, but you don't pay taxes on the profit you make inside the plan or on the money you take out of the plan. Thus a 6 percent return inside a Roth IRA is a 6 percent after-tax return. College savings accounts, called *529 savings plans*, are similar to Roth IRAs in that after-tax dollars are invested in the plan, which then grow tax free as long as the proceeds are used to pay for educational expenses.

Table 10.1 Three Ways to Invest $2,000 of Your
Income, 50 Percent Tax Bracket

	Defer taxes by investing $2,000 in IRA that earns 6% before taxes	*Pay $1,000 tax and invest $1,000 in non-IRA that earns 6% after taxes*	*Pay $1,000 tax and invest $1,000 in Roth IRA that earns 6% before taxes*
Initial value	$2,000	$1,000	$1,000
Value after 24 years before taxes	$8,000	$4,000	$4,000
Value after 24 years after taxes	$4,000	$4,000	$4,000

These tax shelters are very appealing because they allow your investments to be lightly taxed, or not taxed at all. Your home can also be a tax shelter. That's why we call it an HRA, a Home Retirement Account. When you buy a home with an amortized mortgage, part of your monthly payment repays your loan and therefore builds up equity in your home. Month after month, you pay off your loan until the loan is fully repaid. This is very similar to saving money in a Roth IRA.

Suppose, for example, that you buy a home for $400,000 with an $80,000 down payment and a 30-year mortgage at a 6 percent interest rate. Think of your home as a bank account and think of your principal payments as bank deposits. Your principal payments are savings that build up equity in your home, the same way savings deposited in a bank build up your bank account.

Even if home prices don't increase, your wealth is increasing as your mortgage is paid off. In the very unlikely case where the home is still worth $400,000 thirty years after you bought it, it will be all yours and your home equity will have increased from

$80,000 to $400,000. This is a 5.5 percent annual increase in your wealth and is tax-free.

If home prices increase, your wealth will grow even more. Suppose home prices increase by an average of 3 percent a year, roughly the rate of inflation over the past several years. If so, a house that sells for $400,000 today will sell for $970,000 thirty years from now. Relative to your initial $80,000 down payment, this is an 8.7 percent annual rate of increase.

Over the past 30 years, home prices in the United States have increased by 6 percent a year. What if that is true for the next 30 years? Now your house will be worth $2.3 million, and your annual rate of increase will be 11.8 percent.

The overall return from your home investment also depends on your home dividends, which are your rent savings and tax benefits minus your mortgage payments and other expenses. A lifetime of home dividends is also part of your HRA. Remember the Fishers, Indiana, example in Chapter 3, "Now is a Good Time to Own a Home." Most of the increase in the homeowner's wealth came from investing the home dividends. The details obviously vary from house to house and person to person. Our point is simply that you should think of your home as a retirement account.

An HRA is similar to a retirement account in that you can use your HRA to pay your bills when you are retired. If you have an IRA, you can take money out of your IRA to pay your rent. If you have an HRA, you don't have to pay rent because you own your home. Similarly, you can use a lifetime of home dividends to pay for golf clubs and cruises when you are retired. You can also use your HRA as collateral for home equity loans to support your lifestyle.

In some ways, your HRA is even better than an IRA. Most retirement accounts have limits on the amount you can invest each year; an HRA doesn't. Most retirement accounts have minimum distribution requirements that force you to withdraw money after you reach a specified age; an HRA doesn't.

Life Is a Journey: From Porterville & Indio to Thatcher

Bill Davis grew up in Porterville, a small town in California's Great Central Valley. He was valedictorian of his high-school class —a class of 12 students. Helen Nance grew up in Indio, a small California desert town that is perhaps best known for its annual date festival, which features camel races and a surprising variety of foods made with dates—including date ice cream.

Bill and Helen married in 1942 and bought their first home in 1946: a 900-square-foot, 2-bedroom home, 100 yards from a railroad track in Buena Park, a modest suburban community that was close to Bill's job in the southern California aerospace industry. They paid $4,000 for this home with a $500 down payment and a $3,500 mortgage at a 4.7 percent interest rate.

By 1954, they had four children, ages 9, 3, 1, and newborn. They needed a bigger home and Bill's growing salary allowed them to afford one. They bought a new 3-bedroom, 2-bath tract home in La Habra, another quiet southern California town. They sold their Buena Park home for $8,000 and paid $13,000 for their new home.

The Davises raised their family in this home until all their children were grown and Bill and Helen had grown tired of how crowded and congested southern California had become—not at all like their childhood homes in Porterville and Indio. In 1990, Bill retired and they sold their La Habra home for $275,000 and bought a $25,000 condominium on Golf Course Road in Thatcher, Arizona. Bill taught at the local community college and played golf almost every day; Helen took photography classes at the community college and took pictures of Arizona's natural beauty.

Bill's pension from his aerospace employer, his Social Security payments, and the $250,000 they netted from selling their home in La Habra and buying a home in Thatcher provided them with a secure, comfortable retirement.

Their lifetime of homeownership had turned a $500 investment into a $275,000 retirement nest egg (a 15 percent annual rate of return). In addition, the rent they saved every year for decades paid for all four children to go to college. Their home was the best investment they ever made.

Raid Your IRA to Pay Off Your Mortgage?

Some well-known financial advisers say that paying off your mortgage is better than putting money in a retirement plan. Some even say that you should take money out of your retirement plan and pay the penalties for doing so in order to pay off your mortgage. Are they right?

Let's compare the return on your retirement plan with the return from paying off your mortgage. As explained earlier, your retirement plan's return is an after-tax return if you have a Roth IRA or if you have the same tax rate when you put money into a tax-deferred plan and when you withdraw money from it. The after-tax return from paying off your mortgage is the interest rate you are paying on this mortgage taking into account the fact that it is tax deductible.

For example, suppose you have a mortgage with a 6 percent interest rate and you can deduct the interest from your taxable income. If your federal tax rate is 33 percent, Table 10.2 shows that your after-tax mortgage rate is 4.02 percent. Therefore, the after-tax return from paying off your mortgage is 4.02 percent. If you can do better than this with your IRA (and you need a new financial advisor if you can't), then keep your mortgage and keep putting money into your retirement plan. Don't take money out of your retirement plan, especially if there are penalties for doing so, to pay down your mortgage.

Shortchanging your IRA so that you can pay off your mortgage is seldom a good idea.

Table 10.2 After-Tax Mortgage Rate

Federal	Before-Tax Mortgage Rate				
Tax Rate	4%	5%	6%	7%	8%
10%	3.60	4.50	5.40	6.30	7.20
15%	3.40	4.25	5.10	5.95	6.80
25%	3.00	3.75	4.50	5.25	6.00
28%	2.88	3.60	4.32	5.04	5.76
33%	2.68	3.35	4.02	4.69	5.36
35%	2.60	3.25	3.90	4.55	5.20

Reverse Annuity Mortgages

In a conventional mortgage, you borrow money to buy a home and then make monthly payments to repay the loan. In a reverse annuity mortgage, you already own your home and you borrow money monthly for several years, at the end of which you repay your loan. A reverse mortgage is typically repaid when the borrower passes away or sells the home.

In a standard home-equity loan, you use the equity in your home as collateral for the loan. A reverse mortgage is essentially a series of monthly home equity loans. A single, large home equity loan might be appropriate if you need a substantial amount of cash for a remodeling project, to pay college expenses, or to pay off credit-card debt. A reverse mortgage might be appropriate if you need monthly income to pay for food, utilities, and other recurring expenses.

The obvious candidates for a reverse mortgage are retired people who don't have much income to live on and don't own much other than the house they live in. They don't want to sell their home, but they would like to use some of the equity they have built up in their home to improve their standard of living.

Grandma Ford

Gretchen Ford lives in a modest house in West University Place, Texas. West University Place is a small city in the Houston metropolitan area close to Rice University (hence its name). West U was once a working-class neighborhood but has since become very fashionable. Many professionals have moved into West University Place and either completely remodeled the original cottages or torn them down and built large 2-story houses.

Mrs. Ford is now in her 80s and has lived in her house for over 50 years; her husband died several years ago and her son lives 15 minutes away. To everyone in the neighborhood, Mrs. Ford is known as Grandma Ford. Whenever anyone parks in front of her house, she comes out to greet them (usually wearing a bathrobe) and to ask what they are doing in the neighborhood. She is quick to smile and offer directions, even if she doesn't always recognize her neighbors. Although her home has become very valuable because of its great location, Grandma Ford has no savings and lives on her Social Security income. She sometimes forgets to pay her bills and might run a little short of money at the end of the month.

Piles of neatly stacked newspapers are throughout her house, carefully placed so that she can go from room to room walking a narrow path between the newspaper stacks. The backyard has a lot of trash because Grandma Ford sometimes takes out the trash by tossing it out the back door. Leaves falling from tree branches above the house composted on the roof and a 5-foot tree grew on her roof, with roots that grew into the ceiling and let rainwater drip into the laundry room.

Every once in a while, Grandma Ford's son will stop by—apparently to see if she is still alive, because he will inherit the house when Grandma Ford dies. He doesn't give her money to buy food and he doesn't help her clean up her property, but neighbors bring food by, took the tree off her roof, and periodically clean her backyard. Grandma Ford doesn't let them touch her newspapers because she hasn't finished reading them.

The paradox here is that Grandma Ford is living in a home that is worth hundreds of thousands of dollars, but she can't afford to buy decent food or to pay someone to help her with household chores. She is the person for whom the reverse annuity mortgage was invented. Suppose she wanted to receive $1,000 a month and the interest rate is 6 percent. If she were to live past 100, she would owe the bank about $450,000 after 20 years, which would take a bite out of her estate, but certainly not take all of it. Who could object? Only her son, who would inherit less when Grandma Ford dies. Grandma Ford is actually a wealthy woman who could be living a much more comfortable life. The question is whether she should borrow money at a 6 percent interest rate to live more comfortably. If her son doesn't want his mother to borrow at 6 percent, then he can give her some money each month and help take care of her and the property he is waiting to inherit. If he isn't willing to help, then Grandma Ford should use a reverse annuity mortgage to help herself.

What Do I Owe You?

The amount you can borrow each month with a reverse mortgage depends on the amount of equity in the home (the more equity the better), your age (the older the better), and current interest rates (the lower the better). The monthly income is set so that the lender can be almost certain that the cumulative debt is less than the equity in the home when the borrower moves or dies. Table 10.3 shows some illustrative calculations using a 6 percent interest rate.

Table 10.3 Amount Owed at the End of a Reverse Annuity
Mortgage with a 6 Percent Interest Rate

Horizon	Monthly Income		
	$400	$600	$800
10 years	$65,306	$97,959	$130,613
20 years	$182,258	$273,387	$458,128
30 years	$391,703	$587,554	$783,405

The amounts owed after 30 years are a bit daunting because of the power of compound interest. However, the value of the home will also presumably increase over time. If the value of the home increases by 3 percent a year, its value will be 35 percent higher after 10 years, 81 percent higher after 20 years, and 143 percent higher after 30 years.

RAMed by a RAM?

The owner of a real estate firm in Washington, D. C., once wrote a book in which he warned elderly homeowners that they could get "RAMed" by a reverse annuity mortgage. As an example, he looked at a reverse mortgage with a 13 percent interest rate (this was back in the 1980s, a time of double-digit interest rates). The homeowner would receive $145 a month for 15 years (180 months) for a total of $26,100 (180 × $145 = $26,100), but would owe $80,000 at the end of 15 years. The author wrote, "Yes, the homeowner gets $26,100 (much less if inflation is figured in) and owes $80,000 in 15 years!"

We are not sure why inflation should be figured in. Inflation does reduce the purchasing power of the $145 monthly income, but inflation also reduces the purchasing power of the $80,000 that is owed at the end of 15 years. This realtor seems shocked that the homeowner pays $80,000 and only gets $26,100. Well, here's a news flash: If you borrow money, you have to pay back what you borrowed plus interest! The homeowner must pay interest on this $26,100 and consequently pays back more than $26,100; with a 13 percent interest rate and no payments made for 15 years, the total owed works out to be $80,000.

Do you recognize our old friend, the total-payments error? This realty owner adds up the amounts received over 15 years and compares this to the amount paid at the end of 15 years as if a dollar today is the same as a dollar 15 years from now. Unless the interest rate is zero (fat chance!), you will always pay back more money than you borrow. The relevant question is simply whether you want to borrow at the current interest rate. For elderly persons living in valuable homes but struggling to pay their bills, the answer may well be yes.

The Bottom Line

1. Your home can be a retirement account that accumulates wealth to support you during retirement.
2. An HRA is tax advantaged because the rent savings and home appreciation are not taxed or lightly taxed (if the value of your home soars, you might have to pay a capital gains tax).
3. Don't raid your IRA to pay off your mortgage.
4. If you own your home, you can use a reverse annuity mortgage to support your retirement.

11

Selling Your Home

In Chapter 4, "Finding a Home and Closing the Deal," we discussed several aspects of buying a home. There may also come a time when you want to sell your home.

One scenario is that you think home prices are about to fall. Your plan is to sell your home and rent for a while, planning to buy a home again after prices fall. We are not enthusiastic about this strategy. It is hard to time the stock market and it is difficult to time the real estate market. We have seen too many people bail out of stocks at the bottom and jump back in at the top. In fact, we know one person whose timing is so excruciatingly bad that we use him as a contrary indicator. When he sells, we buy; when he buys, we sell. It is just as useful to know someone who is always wrong about stocks as it is to know someone who is always right.

We have also seen too many people wait to buy a home, hoping that prices will come down, only to find that home prices go up so much that they can no longer afford to buy the home they want. We have also seen people sell their homes and rent, planning to buy again after prices collapse, only to find that home prices increase so much that they can no longer afford to buy the home they used to live in.

There are other, more compelling reasons to sell your home. Your income has gone up and you can afford something nicer than the starter home you currently live in. You now have three children and your 2-bedroom, 1-bath home is no longer big enough for your family. Your company has transferred you from Portland to Austin and you don't want to commute. You've quit your job in Austin and taken a job in Portland and you can't take your home with you. You've remarried and your new spouse is unnerved by the traces of your ex that permeate your home. Your children have grown up and you don't want to take care of a 4-bedroom, 3-bath home.

This chapter discusses several issues related to selling your home. As usual, we aren't going to talk about dotting i's and crossing t's. Instead, we discuss some important and maybe not-so-obvious issues.

Home Dividends, Again

You have seen in earlier chapters how home-dividend calculations can help you decide whether a home is likely to be a good investment. If the answer is yes, then you should consider buying and might even pay more than suggested by comps to close the deal. On the other hand, if a home is likely to be a poor investment, you should hesitate about buying this home unless you can get a substantial concession on the price or perhaps an attractive creative financing arrangement.

Home-dividend calculations can also be useful if you are on the other side of the table, thinking about selling your home. If your home is an attractive investment because of the generous home dividends, you might be less willing to budge on the price. You might even use your home-dividend calculations to try to persuade buyers to pay more than suggested by comps, as did the Royers in the example discussed in Chapter 9. If you can't get a good price, maybe you should hold on to your home and rent it out.

If you are thinking about selling and the poor home dividends make this home an unattractive investment, you might be more willing to unload it—maybe throw in the washer and dryer to clinch a sale with a serious buyer.

To sum up, knowing the home dividends and investment value of your home gives you extra information that can help you make better decisions about the sale price.

Curb Appeal

Everyone knows that first impressions are important in personal relationships. They are important in real estate, too. Real estate agents talk about curb appeal, which is the emotions buyers feel when they first drive up to a house. If the home looks great, buyers will walk in the front door with a positive attitude; if a home looks so-so or worse, buyers will enter the home looking for reasons to say no; some won't even bother getting out of their cars.

So, make the front of your home as inviting as possible. Mow the lawn, trim the trees, pick up debris, plant cheerful flowers, and give the front of the house a fresh coat of paint. And, oh yeah, no cars on blocks, please.

Once buyers are out of their cars, you still need to get them into the house. Remove the dog poop from the sidewalk. Clear the spiderwebs away from the front porch. Make sure the front door opens smoothly. (We know a couple who always entered their home through the attached garage. When they put their home on the market, they discovered that the front door was sagging a bit on its hinges. The first time the realtor showed the home to potential buyers, she had to lower her shoulder and ram the door to open it. We're not making this up!)

Once the buyers make it through the front door, what do they see? Well, what would you want to see? A dark hallway? Gruesome pictures on the wall? Dirty clothes on the floor? Two barking German Shepherds? Walk into your own home and imagine that you are entering it for the first time. Would you say, "Wow, what a wonderful home?" If not, why not? Fix whatever needs to be fixed so that buyers will say, "Wow!"

Realtors never want the sellers around when a home is being shown to prospective buyers. Their presence makes the buyers nervous and makes it more difficult for buyers to imagine themselves living in the home.

Realtors have all sorts of strategies to make a home seem more inviting. One is to turn on all the lights to make the house appear bright and cheery. We know a Pennsylvania realtor who turns on soft music, has a fire going in the fireplace, and puts freshly baked bread on the stove. If the home is close enough to a major road to hear commuter traffic, some realtors only show the home on weekends. Ditto if the home is close enough to a school for noisy children to be a nuisance. If the home has a mosquito problem, some realtors don't show the home at dusk.

Clean It Up!

Less clutter makes a house look roomier and cleaner. Nobody wants to move into a house that seems small, unclean, or neglected. It seems crazy, but get as much as you can off of the kitchen counter—the coffee maker, the toaster oven, even the salt and pepper shakers. Put everything in drawers, cupboards, and the garage. Do the same in every bathroom. Empty all the trash cans and hide them.

Most sellers weed through their belongings after they sell the house and before they move. If you are going to do that, why not do it before you put your home on the market? Go through all your stuff and decide what you are not going to take with you. Then have a garage sale or give it away. This will unclutter your house and make it easier to sell. Plus, it will be one less thing to do when preparing for your move.

The Murnanes had bought a new house, but not yet sold their old house. The realtor told them to move half their stuff either to their garage or to the new house. The garage is usually safe because it is the last thing most buyers look at and by then they've made up their mind. Sellers can also lock the garage if they uncluttered their home by filling up the garage. The Murnanes were told not to empty the house completely, because an empty house looks weird and suggests a desperate seller. The realtor also had the Murnanes buy new kitchen towels, bathroom towels, and bedspreads. The Murnanes didn't ever use these, they just put them out whenever their house was being shown to potential buyers.

Pictures on the Wall

Should you leave your family photos out? We don't know. One school of thought is that you want prospective buyers to imagine the home as their own, which is hard to do when the seller's family photos are documenting the many years they spent in the house. On the other hand, we know a New York family with a Caucasian wife, Chinese husband, and three daughters, who left their family pictures on the wall because the paint behind the pictures had not faded as much as the rest of the wall. The first family to look at the house was—you guessed it—a family with a Caucasian wife, Chinese husband, and three daughters. They decided that this house was meant to be theirs, so they made a full-price offer that evening which was quickly accepted.

Loss Aversion

Figure 11.1 shows that the average price of condominiums in Boston nearly tripled between 1982 and 1988 and then fell by almost 35 percent over the next five years.

Boston Condo Prices

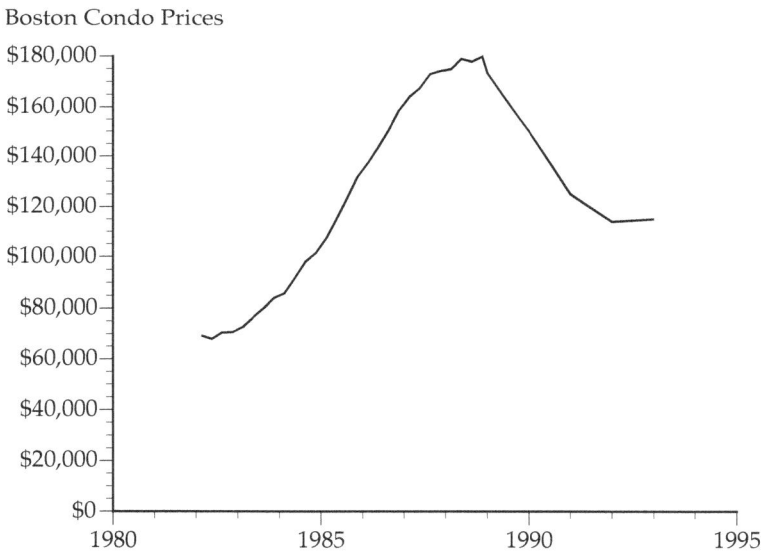

Figure 11.1 Boston condominium prices
fell 35% between 1988 and 1993

Many people who bought condos in the late 1980s and wanted to sell in the early 1990s would have had to sell their condos for a loss. A study of the Boston condo market in the 1990s found that sellers facing losses tended to ask much higher prices than did sellers who were not facing losses. The condos with losses consequently stayed on the market longer, with the sellers eventually either pulling their condos off the market or selling years later when condo prices had recovered. These homeowners were evidently so averse to taking a loss on their condos that they would rather not sell than sell for a loss. They were also using their purchase price as an anchor for what they thought their condos were worth.

Figure 11.2 shows that the number of sales dropped dramatically in the early 1990s.

Boston Condo Prices

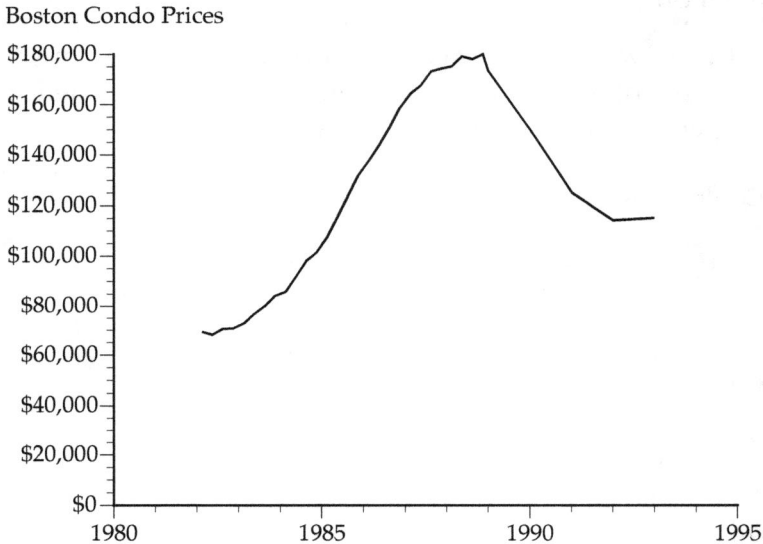

Figure 11.2 Boston condominium sales
fell 47% between 1988 and 1993

This loss aversion is irrational because the market price of a condo is what it is, regardless of what the owner originally paid for it. There is no reason why condos that were purchased at a time of high prices should be worth more than condos purchased at a time of low prices. Certainly it makes no difference to buyers. If it makes a difference to sellers, they pay for their irrationality by not being able to sell their condos.

It is not just Boston condo owners who suffer from loss aversion. Oftentimes when home prices rise and then soften, home prices do not fall much but the volume of sales drops dramatically. Sellers are reluctant to sell their homes for less than they paid for them or for less than recently observed prices. So, the volume of home sales drops sharply, but prices only drop slightly.

There is loss aversion in the stock market, too. Investors have to pay taxes on the profits they "realize" by selling a stock; they can also deduct losses they realize. A sensible strategy is to sell stocks that have gone down in price for the tax benefits and hold onto stocks that have appreciated in order to avoid paying capital gains taxes. Yet, many investors are reluctant to sell a stock for less than they paid for it because that would be an admission that they made a bad investment. (There are two kinds of investors: those who have made mistakes and those who are liars.)

So they hold on to their losers, hoping that the price will recover someday. Even finance professors are susceptible to this fallacy. A notable professor once bragged to a colleague that he had made 25 percent a year during the terrible bear market in the 1970s. Surely, the colleague asked, you must have bought some stocks that went down? He nearly fell out of his chair laughing when the finance professor replied, "Yes, but I haven't sold them yet!"

Waiting for the Right Price

The Lees accepted a job in Colorado and put their Virginia home on the market. Because they didn't need to move to Colorado for another three months, the Lees set their price high and decided that they wouldn't accept a penny less. Days, weeks, and then months passed with only two offers, both of which the Lees considered insulting.

And then three months were up. Mr. Lee took his daughters to Colorado so that they could start school and Mrs. Lee stayed in their Virginia house, keeping it clean and occupied while she waited for the right price.

The Lees had enough money for a down payment on a house in Colorado even without selling their Virginia house, so they bought a house in Colorado. Another nine months passed. Finally, a full year after putting their Virginia house on the market, they were able to sell it for their asking price. It took a while, but the market finally caught up with their price.

The Lees were delighted that they got their asking price, but it was a very expensive wait. For nine months, they were paying mortgages, property taxes, maintenance, and other expenses on two homes. Plus, they were living separately. The Lees paid dearly for their stubbornness.

If you are serious about selling your home, you need to be realistic about the price. You won't get a higher price because you paid more for your home than your neighbors paid for theirs.

Our Price Is Firm, But the Terms Are Negotiable

Rueben and Mary Bravo moved to Houston in 1981 and had to sell their home in Philadelphia. Their asking price was $100,000, but mortgage rates were a staggering 18 percent and buyers were scarce. The Bravos didn't want to reduce their asking price, so they agreed to owner-finance by lending the buyer $80,000 for 30 years at a 12 percent interest rate. This owner-financing was equivalent to a large price cut, in that the lower interest rate reduced the monthly payments substantially, from $1,206 to $823. The Bravos would have had to reduce the price of their home by more than 25 percent, from $100,000 to $74,601, in order for the buyers to get such low monthly payments with an 18 percent mortgage.

Before sellers agree to a below-market loan, they should consider the possibility that it might be less expensive to cut the price than to owner-finance.

The Bottom Line

1. Home-dividend calculations can help you decide if selling your home is financially advantageous.
2. You will sell your home faster if you give the outside of your home curb appeal and unclutter the inside.
3. If you are serious about selling, be realistic about the price.
4. Buyers don't care what you paid for your home and you shouldn't let it influence your asking price.

AFTERWORD

We have discussed many aspects of buying, owning, and selling the home you live in. We've also discussed some important ways of getting the most value out of your home. We wrote this book for people who plan to live in their homes for several years; who want to know if it is still a good idea to be a homeowner; and who want to make buying, financing, remodeling, refinancing, and selling decisions that will allow their homes to be engines to financial prosperity.

We are convinced that real estate will continue to be one of the most appealing ways for you to achieve financial security and, along the way, to enjoy—indeed love—your investment in ways that you could never love stocks, bonds, and bank accounts.

You do not need to be a home flipper or a landlord to be a wise and successful real estate investor. You do not have to pay unconscionable sums to motivational speakers who will try to persuade you to risk your life savings on speculative real estate gambles. You can simply be a sensible homeowner who enjoys the home you live in and the financial rewards that go with homeownership.

Build up equity in your home and invest your home dividends wisely. If you do, your home will be the best investment you will ever make.

Appendix A

An Owner-Occupied
Home in Fishers, Indiana

Chapter 3, "Now is a Good Time to Own a Home" discussed the Nelson's purchase of a home in Fishers, Indiana, in 2005. To calculate their home dividend, we made a list of the annual benefits and expenses associated with owning the home: the rent savings, mortgage payment, property taxes, the tax savings from the tax deductibility of mortgage interest and property taxes, homeowner's insurance instead of renter's insurance, any utilities they would have to pay as owners they wouldn't have to pay as renters, and maintenance.

Table A.1 shows the numbers we used. This appendix explains how we determined these numbers.

Table A.1 After-Tax Home Dividend for a Home in Fishers

Income and Expenses	Dollar Amount
Rent savings	$15,000
Mortgage payment	−$7,522
Property tax	−$2,619
Tax savings	$2,447
Insurance	−$334
Utilities	$0
Maintenance	−$1,350
Home dividend	$5,622

Rent savings. It would cost the Nelsons $1,250 a month ($15,000 a year) to rent a comparable house; so the purchase of this house saves them $15,000 a year in rent. We entered this $15,000 in the first row of Table A.1.

Mortgage payment. In the summer of 2005, the interest rate on a 30-year, fixed-rate mortgage was 5.7 percent, and the Nelson's mortgage payments were $626.83, or $7,522 a year, which we entered on the second row of Table A.1 with a negative sign because this is an expense.

Property tax. In Indiana, property-tax rates are set each year to raise enough revenue to pay for government spending. We estimated that the tax rate on this home would be 2.7 percent. Indiana residents are eligible for a $3,000 homeowner exemption if they have a mortgage. They are also eligible for a homeowner exemption of $35,000 or half the value of the house, whichever is less, if this home is the owner's primary residence. The 2.7 percent tax is levied on the difference between the assessed value and homeowner exemptions:

$$\text{property tax} = 0.027(\$135,000 - \$3,000 - \$35,000) = \$2,619$$

We entered this $2,619 tax with a negative sign in the third row of Table A.1.

Tax savings. Of the $7,522 in mortgage payments made the first year, $6,120 is interest on the loan and $7,522–$6,120 = $1,402 is a partial repayment of the original amount borrowed. The Nelsons can include the $6,120 in interest and the $2,619 in property taxes as an itemized deduction on their federal income tax return. Because they are in a 28 percent federal income tax bracket, this saves them 0.28($6,120+$2,619) = $2,447 in federal income taxes.

Indiana residents do not deduct mortgage interest from their state taxable income, but they are allowed to deduct up to $2,500 of either property taxes or rent from taxable income. Here, the Nelsons would be able to deduct $2,500 either way, so there is no net gain or loss in their state income taxes from owning a home instead of renting. We entered the $2,447 federal tax savings in the fourth row in Table A.1 with a positive sign because it is a benefit.

Insurance. The annual cost of homeowner's insurance is $508 for this house; if the Nelsons were renting instead, they would pay $174 for renter's insurance. We entered the difference, $508–$174 = $334, with a negative sign in the fifth row in Table A.1.

Utilities. We assumed that the Nelsons would incur the same expenses for their telephone, electricity, gas, and other utilities if they were renting. So, there is no difference here between buying and renting, and we entered $0 in the sixth row in Table A.1.

Maintenance. We estimated that annual maintenance expenses would be around 1 percent of the value of the house; here, 0.01×$135,000 = $1,350, which we entered in the seventh row of Table A.1.

Home dividend. Adding up all the entries, the bottom line is a positive home dividend of $5,622.

A Rental Home
in Fishers, Indiana

Chapter 9, "Rental Properties and Vacation Homes" discussed the purchase of a home in Fishers, Indiana, in 2005 as a rental property. This appendix explains how we determined the numbers we used in that example.

If you own the home you live in, your rental saving is what it would cost to rent this home; if you rent a home to someone else, you receive rental income. The crucial difference is that homeowners don't pay taxes on their rent savings, but landlords pay taxes on their rental income (minus expenses). So, if a home is going to be rented out, we need to list the tax-deductible expenses and determine the taxes (if any) that need to be paid. Table B.1 shows the rental income and lists the tax-deductible expenses. We explain below how we came up with these numbers.

Table B.1 Taxable Income for a Rental Home in Fishers

Income and Expenses	Dollar Amount
Rental income	$15,000
Interest portion of mortgage payment	−$6,120
Property tax	−$3,564
Insurance	−$612
Utilities	$0
Maintenance	−$1,350
Depreciation	−$3,682
Taxable income	−$328

Interest portion of mortgage payments. We assume that the mortgage rate does not depend on whether the buyer lives in the house or rents it out to others. As before, the interest rate on 30-year mortgages was 5.7 percent at the time this home was bought, and the mortgage payments work out to be $626.83, or $7,522 a year. Of the $7,522 in mortgage payments made the first year, $6,120 is interest on the loan, which is listed as an expense on the second row of Table B.1.

Property tax. We estimated the tax rate on this home to be 2.7 percent. Indiana residents are eligible for a homeowner exemption of $3,000 if they have a mortgage, plus another homeowner exemption of $35,000 or half the value of the house, whichever is less, if this property is the owner's primary residence. Rental properties and vacation homes are not eligible for the larger exemption. Thus, a landlord pays the following property tax:

$$\text{Property tax} = 0.027(\$135,000 - \$3,000) = \$3,564$$

as compared to a $2,619 property tax if the homeowner lives in the home:

$$\text{Property tax} = 0.027(\$135,000 - \$3,000 - \$35,000) = \$2,619$$

We entered the $3,564 tax with a negative sign in the third row of Table B.1.

Insurance. If the homeowner lives in the home, we considered the difference between homeowner's insurance and renter's insurance. If the home is rented out, we use the cost of rental-property insurance, which is $612. Because this is an expense, we entered $612 with a negative sign in the fourth row of Table B.1.

Utilities. We assume the renter is responsible for all utilities. So, there is no cost for the landlord. We entered $0 in the fifth row of Table B.1.

Maintenance. The maintenance expense is probably higher if the owner rents the home out instead of living in it. Nonetheless, we initially assumed that the annual maintenance expense is the same for both so that we can focus on how the home dividend is affected by the fact that the tax laws are different if the owner lives in the home than if he rents it out. So, as is the case when the owner lives in the home, we assume that maintenance expenses will be 1 percent of the value of the house; here, 0.01×$135,000 = $1,350. Therefore, we entered $1,350 with a negative sign in the sixth row of Table B.1. After analyzing this case in Chapter 9, we increase the maintenance expenses to 2 percent when the house is rented out.

Depreciation. A landlord is allowed to claim a depreciation expense for the structure (but not for the land)—because the structure will eventually wear out, but the land presumably won't. We assume that the value of the structure is equal to 75 percent of the total value: 0.75×$135,000 = $101,250. We depreciate the structure straight line over 27.5 years; this means that the structure is assumed to last 27.5 years and to lose the same fraction of its initial value each year. If the structure is depreciated over 27.5 years, it loses 3.636 percent of its initial value each year: 100/27.5 = 0.03636. The annual depreciation expense is consequently 0.03636×$101,250 = $3,682.

Taxable income. Table B.1 shows that, adding up all the entries, there is a loss for tax purposes. We assume that the owner does not qualify as a real estate professional and does not qualify for the small-investor exception. There is consequently no state or federal tax liability or benefit.

Now that we have the tax bill (zero), we can list all the components of the home dividend in Table B.2. This is a list of the annual benefits and expenses associated with owning the home and renting it out: the rental income, mortgage payment, property taxes, income taxes, rental-property insurance, utilities, and maintenance. Table B.2 shows that the home dividend is positive even though, because of the depreciation expense, there is a loss for tax purposes.

Table B.2 After-Tax Home Dividend for a Rental in Fishers

Income and Expenses	Dollar Amount
Rent savings	$15,000
Mortgage payment	−$7,522
Property tax	−$3,564
Income taxes	$0
Insurance	−$612
Utilities	$0
Maintenance	−$1,350
Home dividend	$1,952

Appendix C

Your Home

Appendix A, "An Owner-Occupied Home in Fishers, Indiana" walked through an example of estimating the first-year home dividend for a home in Fishers, Indiana. This appendix lets you make the same calculations for your own home or a home you are considering buying.

Table C.1 lists the annual benefits and expenses associated with owning a home: the rent savings, mortgage payment, property taxes, the tax savings from the tax deductibility of mortgage interest and property taxes, homeowner's insurance instead of renter's insurance, any utilities you would have to pay as owners that you wouldn't have to pay as renters, and maintenance.

Table C.1 After-Tax Home Dividend for Your Home

Income and Expenses	Dollar Amount
Rent savings	+
Mortgage payment	−
Property tax	−
Tax savings	+
Insurance	−
Utilities	−
Maintenance	−
	————

Home dividend (add the above items)

Rent savings. How much would it cost you to rent this home? Look in newspapers or on the Internet for comparable homes that are for rent in the neighborhood. You can even call a realtor and ask what it would cost to rent an x-bedroom, y-bath home in your neighborhood. Remember to multiply the monthly rent by 12 to get an annual amount, and enter this number in the first row of Table C.1 with a positive sign because this is a benefit.

Mortgage payment. What are the monthly mortgage payments? If you already own the home you are analyzing, you know what your mortgage payments are. If you're thinking about buying a home, you can talk to a bank or use the Internet to estimate what your monthly mortgage payments will be if you buy this home. Multiply the monthly payment by 12 to get the annual payment and enter this number in the second row of Table C.2 with a negative sign because this is an expense.

Property tax. What are the annual property taxes? Enter the annual property tax with a negative sign in the third row of Table C.1.

Tax savings. If you itemize deductions on your federal income tax return, you can include your property taxes with your other itemized deductions on Schedule A. Part of the mortgage payment is interest, which can be another itemized deduction. If you already own this home, your lender sends you an annual statement every January or February that shows these numbers. If you are thinking about buying this home, you can use amortized loan software (there are several on the Internet and you can find one on the *Houseonomics'* accompanying Web site www.houseonomics.com) to determine how much of your annual mortgage payment is interest and how much is principal.

If you know your tax bracket, you can estimate the tax saving by multiplying your tax rate times the sum of your property taxes and mortgage interest. You can get a more accurate number by calculating your most recent federal income taxes twice, with and without using your property taxes and mortgage interest as itemized deductions. The difference in your taxes is your federal tax savings.

If you live in a state that has an income tax, you might be able to use your property taxes and mortgage interest to reduce your state income taxes. Again, a reasonably accurate estimate can be obtained by redoing your most recent tax return with and without the property tax and mortgage interest deduction. If your state has a renter's credit, be sure to omit this from your tax return.

Your total tax savings is the sum of your federal and state tax savings. Once you have your total estimated tax savings, enter this number in the fourth row in Table C.1 with a positive sign because it is a benefit.

Insurance. Your insurance company can tell you how much it would cost for homeowner's insurance if you own this home and how much it would cost for renter's insurance if you rent this home from someone else. The annual insurance expense is the difference between what you would pay for homeowner's insurance and what you would pay for renter's insurance. Enter this difference with a negative sign in the fifth row in Table C.1.

Utilities. Estimate how much more you pay for telephone, electricity, gas, and other utilities if you own this home rather than renting it. Oftentimes, the renter is responsible for all utilities, so there is no difference between buying and renting when it comes to utility bills. If there is a difference, enter this number with a negative sign in the sixth row in Table C.1. Otherwise, enter $0.

Maintenance. We often estimate that annual maintenance expenses will be around 1 percent of the value of the home; you may believe it will be somewhat higher or lower. Enter your estimate with a negative sign in the seventh row of Table C.1.

Home dividend. Add up all the entries and enter the sum in the Home dividend row (the proverbial bottom line). If the rent savings and tax benefit are larger than the mortgage payment and other expenses, your home dividend will be positive; if the benefits are less than the expenses, the home dividend will be negative.

If the home dividend is positive, this home might be a cash cow. Don't despair if the home dividend is initially negative. Sometimes, as with the example of the Lynches in Chapter 3, "Now is a Good Time to Own a Home," the home dividend might initially be negative, but turn positive later on because the rent savings continue to grow but the mortgage payment does not. Still, you need to be careful about homes with a negative home dividend because you don't want to count on appreciating home prices to bail you out of a precarious financial situation.

Regardless of whether the initial home dividend is positive or negative, you can estimate the home dividend in future years by repeating the home dividend calculations and assuming that the various items increase at plausible rates. For example, you might assume that the rent savings, property taxes, homeowner's insurance, utilities, and maintenance all increase at the rate of inflation, say 3 percent a year. If you think that some items might grow at different rates (for example, property taxes might grow faster or slower than the rate of inflation), take this into account.

The mortgage payment will be constant if you have a standard amortized loan with a fixed interest rate. The tax savings will have to be tweaked because the fraction of the mortgage payment that is tax-deductible interest declines as the mortgage is paid off. On balance, the mortgage payment is usually the biggest expense, and the fact that it is constant while the rent savings is increasing causes the home dividend to get better and better as time passes.

First-year rate of return. After determining the first-year home dividend, divide this number by your down payment to get an estimate of your first-year rate of return. For example, if your first-year net home dividend is $2,500 and your down payment is $40,000, then your first-year rate of return is 0.0625:

$$\text{First-year rate of return} = \frac{\text{home dividend}}{\text{down payment}} = \frac{\$2,500}{\$40,000} = 0.0625$$

Multiply this by 100 to get a percentage:

$$100 \times 0.0625 = 6.25 \text{ percent}$$

The first-year rate of return is 6.25 percent.

This rate of return calculation does not take into account the fact that your mortgage payments are building up equity in the home or that the value of this home might be increasing (or decreasing). We are focusing on the home dividend because we want to see if the home dividend alone can justify owning this home. Many readers will find that this is indeed the case—their home is a cash cow. If not, then this home might not be worth the price, no matter what the comps might indicate.

www.ingramcontent.com/pod-product-compliance
Lightning Source LLC
Chambersburg PA
CBHW072342200326
41519CB00015B/3635